The War Atlas

The War Atlas

Armed conflict – Armed peace

Michael Kidron & Dan Smith
A Pluto Press project

Simon & Schuster   New York

Published by Simon & Schuster
A Division of Gulf & Western Corporation
Simon & Schuster Building
Rockefeller Center
1230 Avenue of the Americas
New York, New York 10020

SIMON AND SCHUSTER and colophon
are trade marks of Simon & Schuster

Artwork for maps by Swanston Graphics, Derby, England
Editor and coordinator: Anne Benewick

Text typeset by Capital Setters, London
Printed and bound in Hong Kong by
Mandarin Offset International (HK) Limited

1   2   3   4   5   6   7   8   9   10

Library of Congress Catalog Card No 80-5921
U42.K52 1983
$355^1.009^1$ 04

Contents

Acknowledgements

Included in the list of names below are friends, colleagues, acquaintances, and people we have had contact with only over the telephone. Their views on the issues posed in *The War Atlas* are as various as the places they work. What unites them is that every one of them has given generously of their time, knowledge and intuition. With some we discussed a problem or two just briefly; others spent hours tracking down some arcane detail of the international military order for us, or filling in major gaps in our knowledge and understanding. If they had not let us impose on them, this project would never have been completed. Had we not assumed we could impose on them, we might never have started out. We are deeply grateful to all of them, but, needless to say, none bears any responsibility for flaws in the final product:

Mary Acland-Hood, Bill Arkin, Meg Beresford, András Bereznay, Billie Bielkus, Frank Blackaby, Jonathan Bloch, Christy Campbell, Duncan Campbell, Ian Cuthbertson, Chen Xiaolu, Ted Crawford, Chris Davis, Harry Dean, Jane Dibblin, Christopher Donnelly, Barbara Einhorn, Paul Gerhardt, Niels Peter Gledditsch, Fred Halliday, David Johnston, John Keegan, Signe-Landgren-Bäckström, Andy Little, Moshe Machover, Abdul Minty, Thomas Ohlson, Julian Perry Robinson, S. Rana, Gerald Segal, Ronald Segal, Ric Sissons, Chris Smith, Ron Smith, Malcolm Swanston, Owen Wilkes, Herbert Wulf. Our only regret is that there are some who also aided us to whom we cannot make proper acknowledgements. But they know who they are, and we thank them equally.

Special thanks are due to the librarians of: Imperial War Museum; International Institute of Strategic Studies (Alison Brown, Julie Chamberlain, Cherine Gunaratne, Jane Towell); Royal Institute of International Affairs, Chatham House, London; British Library; British Library of Political and Economic Science; United States Information Service Library; Stockholm International Peace Research Institute Library; RAF Library (Mr Flower); Institute of the Study of Conflict (Jonathan Luxmoore).

Introduction

Woven into world politics there is a self-perpetuating international military order. It is a hierarchy of power based on war, on the threat of war and on permanent preparations for it.

The components of this order are states, armed forces, businesses and enterprises and their political and intellectual supports. They draw their legitimacy, their credibility and their functions from one another. US and Soviet nuclear forces are each justified by reference to the other. The import of sophisticated weapons by one state sustains the arms industry of another. The need for solidity in one military bloc is affirmed by the seeming solidity of the other. Intent on safeguarding 'national security', each contributes to the ambient insecurity on which they all thrive.

Unplanned and unforeseen at its beginnings after the second world war, the international military order is based on relations of mutual threat and reliance, of domination and concession, of conflict and collaboration. They reveal themselves in many ways: in the nuclear arms race, in the international trade in arms, in the confrontation of military blocs, in the high incidence of military rule.

At the apex of the hierarchy are the two superpowers, mutually reinforcing in their competition. Immediately below are their major allies, following their lead more or less willingly, and China. The third tier consists of the major clients – the superpowers' lesser military allies, and the few major states that try to stand aside from the cold war, the non-aligned. For the superpowers, such states are important, but fickle. In the fourth tier come the poorest and weakest states – generally ignored, unless they happen to brush against a larger interest, when they may be bought or bullied as circumstances and tactics dictate.

The states at and near the top of the order have fought most of their wars in the territories of other states. Their mutual relations are regulated by the threat of war rather than by war itself, by insistent preparations for a war that would be suicidal. But cold war has not resolved their conflicts; rather, it has exacerbated and entrenched them. War between them has been deferred, not deterred.

The period since 1945 is one of unremitting but selective warfare: most of the victims have been in the poor countries. These unfortunate hosts to hot wars have often suffered from proxy contests between East and West, but they also know wars along other lines of division – the North-South axis, and regional and civil wars of a more traditional kind.

The ensemble of power relations encompassed by the international military order is not the only force shaping international politics. But, increasingly, it pervades the rest. Economic competition, efforts to defend, extend or, in many countries, create political freedoms, attempts to eliminate malnutrition, curable diseases and other scourges — all feel the constraining hand of the military order.

In this atlas, within the limits of available information, we have set out to depict the global reach of the international military order. We record the wars since 1945, nearly three hundred of them, and their outcomes. We show something of the preparations and potential of a future war. We show the distribution of military hardware and people, the networks of bases and communication stations, the political division of the world, the uses of armed force short of war. The atlas depicts the economic, industrial and commercial aspects of the international military order — military spending, production and trade — and the hierarchy of power which they reveal. We show something of the political and ecological effects of all this activity, and of the growing opposition to it.

But the international military order is not just a dangerous and unstable equilibrium *between* states. It is based on conditions *within* states, where power devolves on those who translate its spirit of universal siege into domestic policies. It reinforces the most regressive aspects of each national society. Waste on a colossal scale, centralised power, inaccessible hierarchies and overblown bureaucracies are complemented by mutual fear and hostility, the glorification of violence, the disabling of dissent and the curtailing of freedom and human dignity. None of these is new, but all owe their contemporary severity to the international military order.

Yet it is not possible to depict with any authority the effects of the international military order on the lives, behaviour and intentions of the mass of people who have no power within it. Little can be said in the format of an atlas about the way armed force is used to organise ethnic and class divisions, or about the way those divisions are used to organise armed force. Still less is known about the lives of women, largely excluded from the military even as their gender stereotypes are included in its ideology. It is beyond our reach to map the relationship between state violence and the distancing of women from power, or men from routine childcare.

The problem is that there is an information order serving social and international power. If knowledge is power, control of information enhances it. Ignorance is weakness, not bliss. That is why the majority of people are hidden from history. That is why the most revealing information is regularly the least available. The control, deployment and, ultimately, the content of information reflect the interests of those who control and deploy social resources.

Military information is an extreme case. Invariably incomplete, it reflects the specialist view of specialised fighting machines as well as their secretiveness. What we show in this atlas is what is *known*, not what *is*. As a result, the atlas very often depicts expressions of military power rather than its reality. It is particularly striking that, for most wars since 1945, there is little reliable information on the numbers of people killed, injured and displaced.

Fortunately, power is not easily conserved. Although the rich and powerful do everything to bend popular perceptions along their own sight paths, they do not always succeed. Now and again, people reject their view. And in that lie opportunity and hope, for not even the international military order can withstand systematic rejection of authority within it.

The maps show the territories of states as generally recognised in mid-1982. Where areas are in dispute — as Namibia, Western Sahara, Palestine, Eritrea, Kurdistan — they are treated in accordance with UN practice. Taiwan is treated as an independent state, although neither the Taiwanese nor the Chinese authorities regard it as such, but as an integral part of China over which both claim sovereignty.

   The maps depict events, statistical information and political judgements. Comments on the information — on its source, reliability and limitations and, in some cases, the methodology which produced it — are included in the *Notes to the Maps* at the end of the atlas. Our sources are indicated cryptically on each map. Full bibliographical details are given in *Sources for the Maps*, also at the end of the atlas.

   Connections and cross-references with maps in other sections of the atlas are suggested in the arrows in the bottom right-hand corner of each map.

A book of this sort comes out of the work of many people. Some of them are recognised in the list of sources. Others, who have given us their personal advice and assistance, are also listed there, except for those — in business, government and the military — who prefer to remain unacknowledged.

   There are some whose full contribution can never be adequately recognised. Without the creativity and commitment of Anne Benewick and Nina Kidron at Pluto Press, the idea of the atlas could not have been transformed into a publishing project, and the project would not have materialised as a book. And without David Williams, who supervised production, and the entire team at Pluto, we would have lacked the unique climate in which this, as so many other ideas, can flourish. Malcolm Swanston and his colleagues have provided inspired cartography and visualisation; and Marsha Austin a sense of colour and design. David Kewley of Pan Books has been unfailingly enthusiastic and helpful.

   We thank them all unreservedly. Above all, we thank each other for stimulus, encouragement and forbearance.

Michael Kidron
Dan Smith

January 1983

Part One: War since 1945

There have been about three hundred wars since 1945. There has been no single day free of war and few islands of tranquillity.

Resort to arms has always been a basic component of power. This does not mean it is inevitable, but it is a major social and political force.

The global reach and destructiveness of modern armed forces are such that war and preparations for war have become a source of worldwide insecurity, and not merely its reflection. War now has the potential, not only to determine, but to terminate social and political organisation. States which seek power and protection by means of nuclear arsenals impose the risk of destroying all life.

Wars since 1945 have been fought for traditional reasons — between states contesting regional power, and between contestants for domestic state power. Both types of war have been fought primarily to influence the reordering of sovereignty which attended the collapse of the old European empires. Initially, they were mainly wars of independence from imperial rule; subsequently, they were fought mainly between the legatees of empire. In their collapse, those old empires, won by war, produced causes for a new round of wars.

Some of these wars have been beneath the interest of the

superpowers. But in the spinning of new webs of international power, many wars have seen the active intervention of the USA and USSR – as armourers, advisers, sponsors, combatants. For behind and within the hot wars has been the cold war between the superpowers and their respective allies. Through all its changes of intensity, this confrontation and the permanent preparation for war it entails have underpinned the international military order and provided its main lines of division.

The extent of war is shown in general terms in *Map 1: A World at War* and in more detail in *Maps 2 to 4: Wars 1945-82*. In *Map 1* we show such information as there is about the immediate victims of war. It is incomplete. The bodies have not all been counted. The less immediate victims – the refugees, the bereaved, the victims of famine caused by war – are similarly un-counted, little acknowledged. They enter the news only when political points can be scored by their suffering, and then only briefly.

The outcome of war is often in doubt. It regularly produces no gain, only loss. And when war does produce a recognisable gain for one side, that must often be defended by further war. The conflicts through which the state of Israel has been constructed, confirmed and expanded are a case in point (see *Map 5: Moah Barzel).*

In one respect in recent years, wars have departed from the classic pattern. Civil wars have been internationalised, not merely by the intervention of a superpower, or of another state acting for a superpower, but by being exported. Some dimensions of this modern variant of war – assassinations, bomb attacks, kidnappings, embassy occupations – are revealed in *Map 6: Caught in the Crossfire*.

In exercises and manoeuvres, armed forces practise constantly for possible future wars (see *Map 7: Practice Makes Perfect*). But they also have other, more immediate functions. Zapad-81 (which means West-81), held in September of that year, was not only the largest Soviet military manoeuvre for many years. It was also extremely significant in the prelude to martial law in Poland, imposed in December 1981. The exercise was extensively reported in the press and on television, in the USSR and Eastern Europe as well as in the West. Such publicity is by no means unusual and is often much of the point.

The possible nature of the war to end war is shown in *Map 8: Ground Zero*. Death and suffering on this kind of scale are hard to imagine, impossible to quantify. Yet the war we depict on the map would use only one-third of the world nuclear stockpile and in that sense would be a limited nuclear war. So far we have been spared, but ours is a warring planet and there can be no guarantee that this good fortune will continue indefinitely.

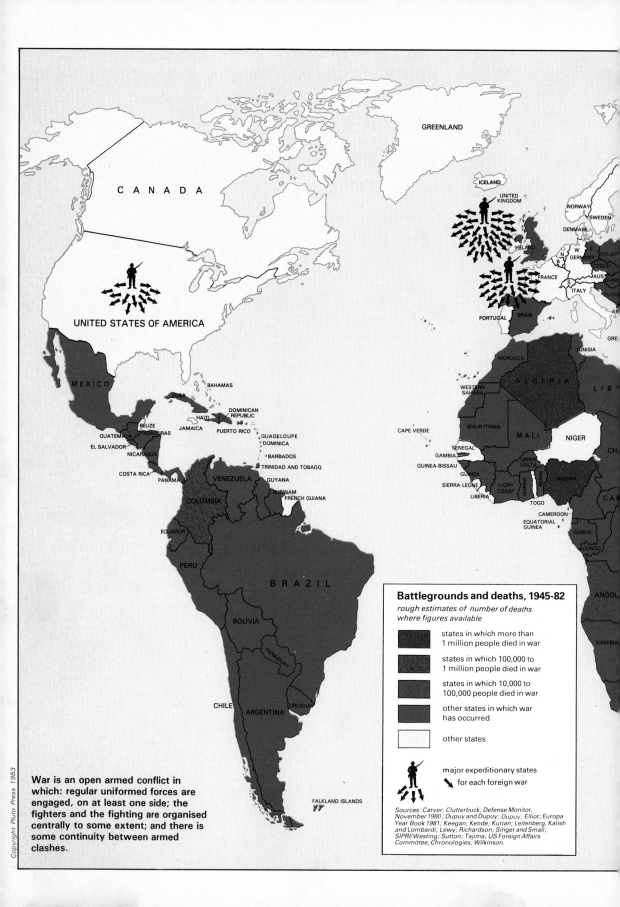

GREENLAND

C A N A D A

ICELAND

UNITED KINGDOM

NORWAY

SWEDEN

IRELAND

DENMARK

W E GERMANY

POLAN

N E B S

CZECH

FRANCE

AUS

HUNG

S W

UNITED STATES OF AMERICA

PORTUGAL

SPAIN

ITALY

YUGO

A

GRE

MOROCCO

TUNISIA

MEXICO

BAHAMAS

CUBA

HAITI

DOMINICAN REPUBLIC

BELIZE

JAMAICA

PUERTO RICO

GUATEMALA

HONDURAS

EL SALVADOR

NICARAGUA

COSTA RICA

PANAMA

VENEZUELA

GUADELOUPE

DOMINICA

BARBADOS

TRINIDAD AND TOBAGO

GUYANA

SURINAM

FRENCH GUIANA

COLOMBIA

ECUADOR

PERU

CAPE VERDE

WESTERN SAHARA

A L G E R I A

LIB

MAURITANIA

M A L I

NIGER

CH

SENEGAL

GAMBIA

UPPER VOLTA

GUINEA-BISSAU

GUINEA

NIGERIA

SIERRA LEONE

IVORY COAST

GHANA

BENIN

LIBERIA

TOGO

CAMEROON

EQUATORIAL GUINEA

CA

GABON

CONGO

B R A Z I L

BOLIVIA

PARAGUAY

ANGOL

NAMIBIA

Battlegrounds and deaths, 1945-82

rough estimates of number of deaths where figures available

- states in which more than 1 million people died in war
- states in which 100,000 to 1 million people died in war
- states in which 10,000 to 100,000 people died in war
- other states in which war has occurred
- other states

major expeditionary states for each foreign war

CHILE

ARGENTINA

URUGUAY

War is an open armed conflict in which: regular uniformed forces are engaged, on at least one side; the fighters and the fighting are organised centrally to some extent; and there is some continuity between armed clashes.

FALKLAND ISLANDS

Sources: Carver; Clutterbuck; Defense Monitor, November 1980; Dupuy and Dupuy; Dupuy; Elliot; Europa Year Book 1981; Keegan; Kende; Kurian; Leitenberg, Kalish and Lombardi; Lewy; Richardson; Singer and Small; SIPRI/Westing; Sutton; Tajima; US Foreign Affairs Committee, Chronologies; Wilkinson.

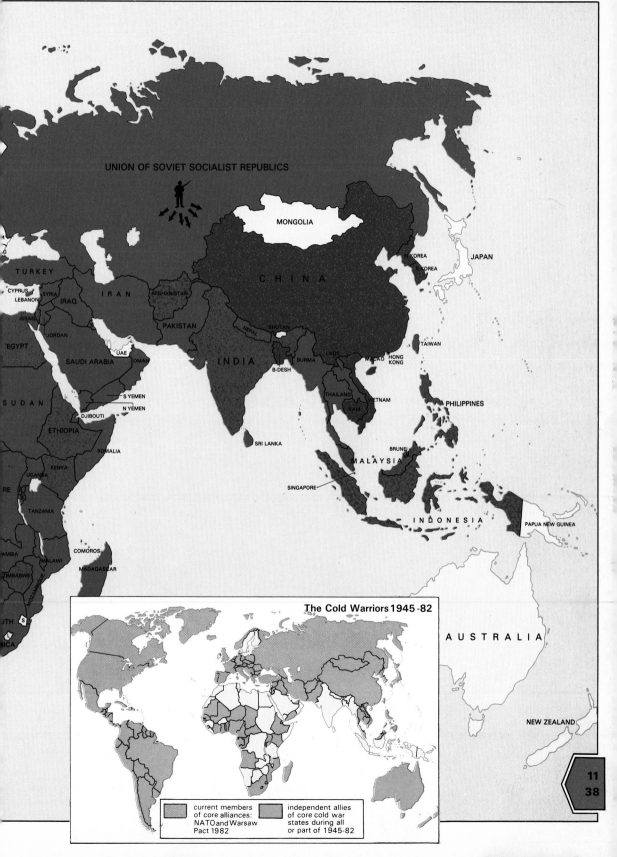

UNION OF SOVIET SOCIALIST REPUBLICS

MONGOLIA

N KOREA

S KOREA

JAPAN

TURKEY

CYPRUS

LEBANON

SYRIA

IRAQ

IRAN

AFGHANISTAN

C H I N A

ISRAEL

JORDAN

EGYPT

PAKISTAN

NEPAL

BHUTAN

TAIWAN

SAUDI ARABIA

UAE

OMAN

I N D I A

B-DESH

BURMA

LAOS

MACAO

HONG KONG

SUDAN

S YEMEN

N YEMEN

DJIBOUTI

THAILAND

VIETNAM

KAM

PHILIPPINES

ETHIOPIA

SRI LANKA

SOMALIA

BRUNEI

M A L A Y S I A

UGANDA

KENYA

SINGAPORE

I N D O N E S I A

PAPUA NEW GUINEA

TANZANIA

COMOROS

MADAGASCAR

A U S T R A L I A

MALAWI

ZIMBABWE

MOZAMBIQUE

The Cold Warriors 1945-82

NEW ZEALAND

current members of core alliances: NATO and Warsaw Pact 1982

independent allies of core cold war states during all or part of 1945-82

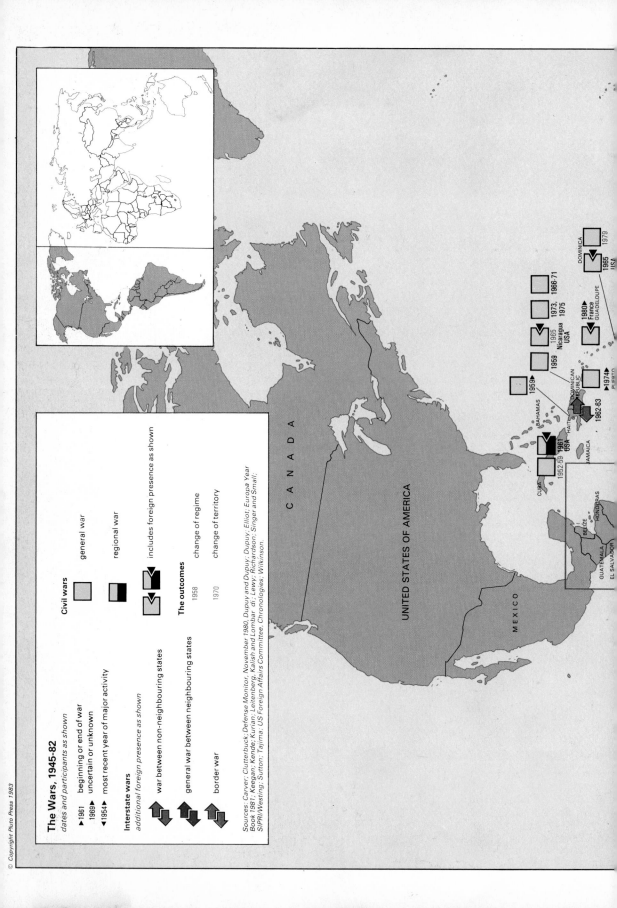

The Wars, 1945-82

dates and participants as shown

Civil wars

▲1961   beginning or end of war
1969▲   uncertain or unknown
1954▼   most recent year of major activity

Interstate wars
additional foreign presence as shown

war between non-neighbouring states

general war between neighbouring states

border war

◻ general war

◼ regional war

⬇ includes foreign presence as shown

The outcomes

1958   change of regime

1970   change of territory

Sources: Carver; Clutterbuck; Defense Monitor, November 1980, Dupuy and Dupuy; Dupuy; Elliot; Europa Year Book 1981; Keegan; Kende; Kurian; Leitenberg, Kalish and Lombar di; Lewy; Richardson; Singer and Small; SIPRI/Westing; Sutton; Tajima; US Foreign Affairs Committee, Chronologies; Wilkinson.

CANADA

UNITED STATES OF AMERICA

MEXICO

BELIZE

GUATEMALA

EL SALVADOR

HONDURAS

CUBA

BAHAMAS

JAMAICA

HAITI

DOMINICAN REPUBLIC

1952-59

1959

1961
USA

1962-63
USA

1959

1965
Nicaragua
USA

1973,
1975

1966-71

1974▼
PUERTO

1980▶
France
GUADELOUPE

1965
IISA

1979

DOMINICA

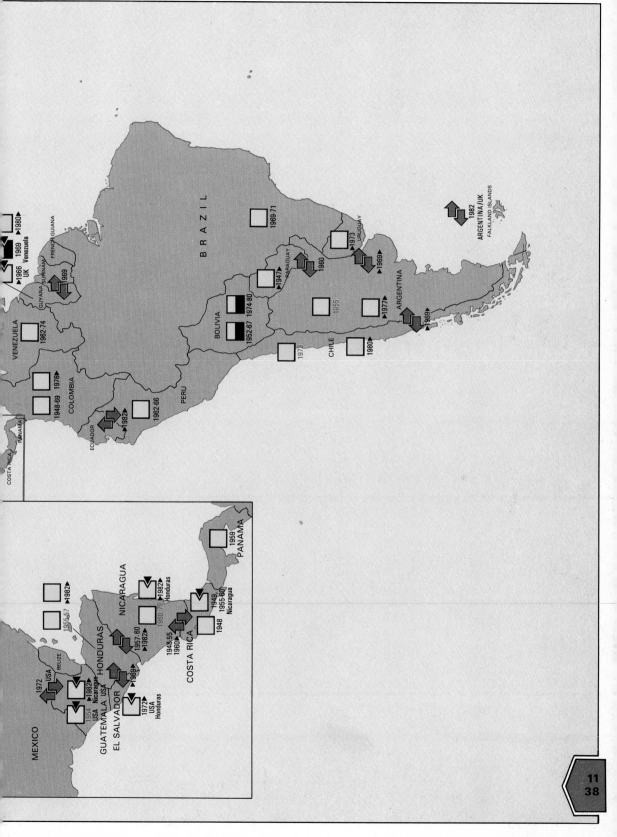

1980

1969 1980▲
UK Venezuela
1966 1969
UK Venezuela
1969

VENEZUELA
1962-74

COLOMBIA
1948-69 1978

PANAMA
COSTA RICA

ECUADOR
1982
1962-66

PERU

BOLIVIA
1974-80
1952-67

BRAZIL
1969-71

1947
1960 PARAGUAY
1973 URUGUAY
1969

1955 CHILE

1973
1977
1980
ARGENTINA
1969

GUYANA
SURINAM
(GUYANA) FRENCH GUIANA

1982
ARGENTINA/UK
FALKLAND ISLANDS

1959
PANAMA

1982
NICARAGUA 1982
Honduras
1960
1957-60
1982
1969
1982
USA Nicaragua
1972
USA
1954
USA
1982
USA Nicaragua
1972
USA Honduras

1982
1955-57

MEXICO
BELIZE
GUATEMALA
HONDURAS
EL SALVADOR
NICARAGUA

1948-55
1960
1948
1949,
1955-60
Nicaragua
COSTA RICA

11
38

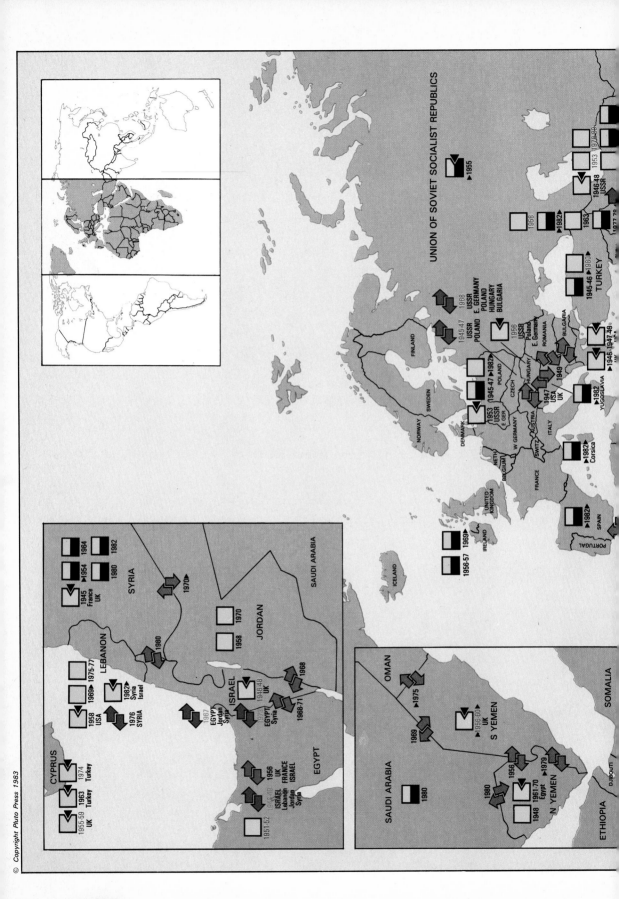

UNION OF SOVIET SOCIALIST REPUBLICS

FINLAND

SWEDEN

NORWAY

DENMARK

NETH

BELGIUM

UNITED KINGDOM

IRELAND

ICELAND

1956-57

1969

W GERMANY

E GER

POLAND

CZECH

AUSTRIA

SWITZ

FRANCE

ITALY

HUNGARY

ROMANIA

BULGARIA

YUGOSLAVIA

1982

1982
Corsica

1982
SPAIN

PORTUGAL

1945-47
USSR
POLAND

1988

1945-47 1982
POLAND

1953
USSR
E GER

1956
USSR
Poland
E. Germany

1947
USA
UK

1949

1945-47
USSR
POLAND
HUNGARY
BULGARIA

1988
USSR
E. GERMANY
POLAND
HUNGARY
BULGARIA

1946-47-49

1946 1947-49

1988

1982

1963

1945-46

1980

1946-48
USSR

1953

1971-88

1977-79

1955

TURKEY

CYPRUS

1955-59
UK

1963
Turkey

1974
Turkey

1958
USA

1969

1975-77

1982
Syria
Israel

1945
France
UK

1954

1970

1964

1980

1982

1976
SYRIA

1946-48
UK

1967
EGYPT
Jordan
Syria

EGYPT
Syria

1968-71

1968

1980

SYRIA

LEBANON

ISRAEL

JORDAN

1970

1958

SAUDI ARABIA

EGYPT

1956
UK
FRANCE
ISRAEL

1948-49
ISRAEL
Lebanon
Jordan
Syria

1951-52

SAUDI ARABIA

OMAN

1975

1969

1956-60
UK
S YEMEN

SOMALIA

1980

1956

1980

1948

1961-70
Egypt

1979

N YEMEN

DJIBOUTI

ETHIOPIA

3. War 1945~82: Europe, Middle East, Africa

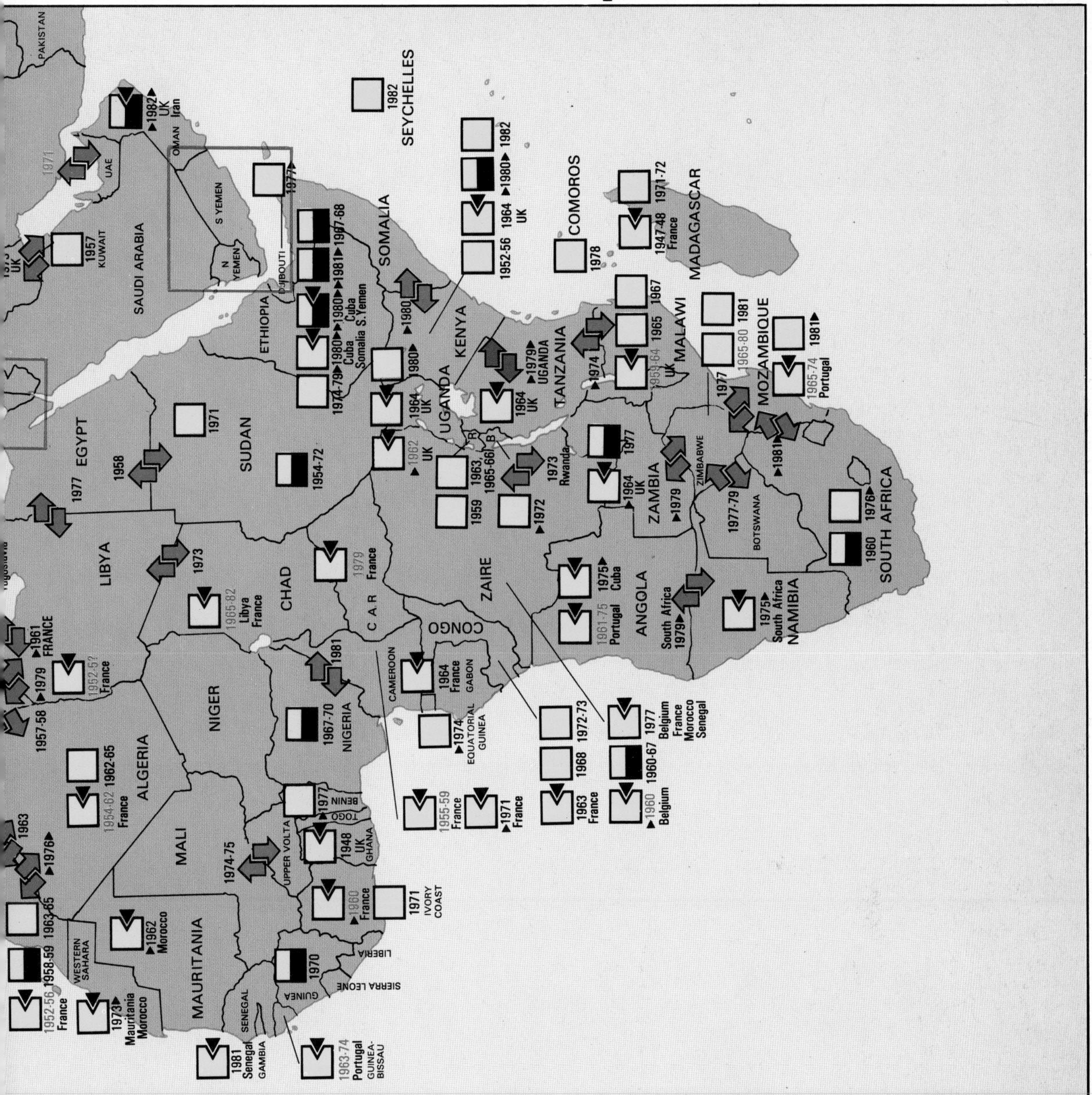

The Wars, 1945-82
dates and participants as shown

▼1980 beginning or end of war
▲1980 uncertain or unknown
►1980► most recent year of major activity

Interstate wars
additional foreign presence as shown

war between non-neighbouring states

general war between neighbouring states

border war

Civil wars

general

regional

includes foreign presence
as shown

The outcomes

1973 change of regime

1946-47 change of territory

*Sources: Carver; Clutterbuck; Defense Monitor,
November 1980; Dupuy and Dupuy; Elliot; Europa
Year Book 1981; Keegan; Kende; Kurian; Leitenberg; Kalish
and Lombardi; Lewy; Richardson; Singer and Small;
SIPRI/Westing; Sutton; Tajima; US Foreign Affairs
Committee, Chronologies; Wilkinson.*

11
38

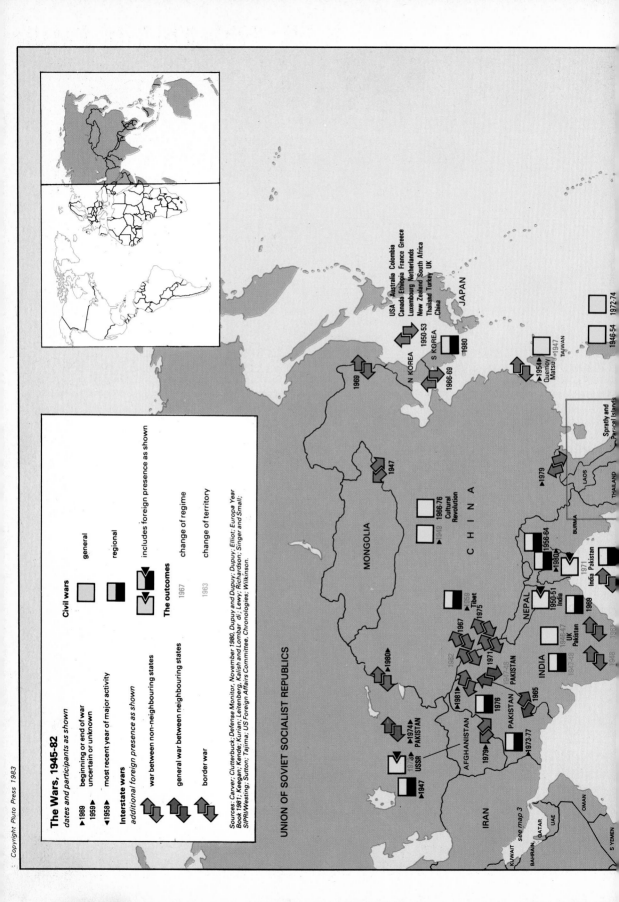

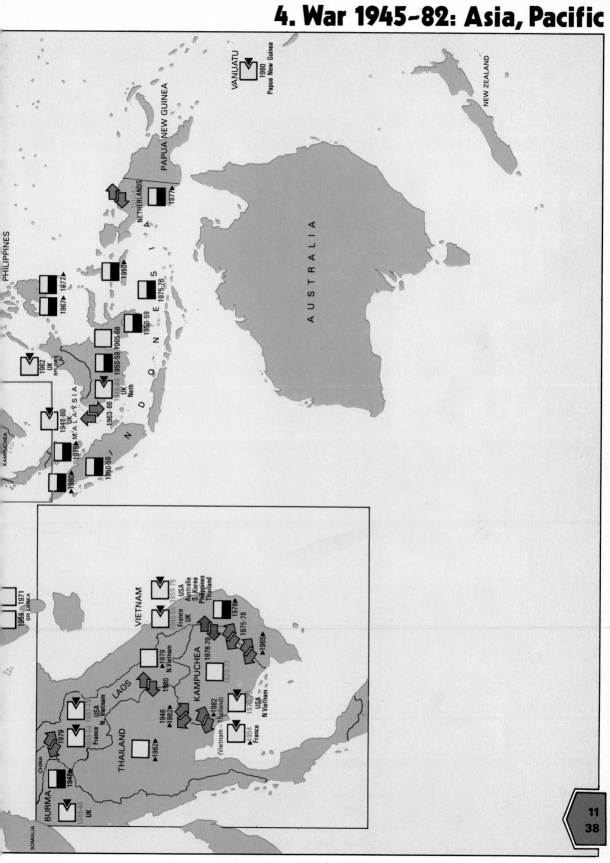

VANUATU
1980
Papua New Guinea

NEW ZEALAND

PAPUA NEW GUINEA

AUSTRALIA

PHILIPPINES

1977▲

1967▶

1977▲

1960▶

NETHERLANDS
1962-62

1977▲

1950-59

1975-76

N   E   S

1962
UK
BRUNEI

1950-59 1965-68

D

1945-49 1950-59
UK
Neth

O

1948-60
UK

1963-66

1975▶

MALAYSIA

1950-59

1980▶

1950-59

N

KAMPUCHEA

SOMALIA

1958 1971
SRI LANKA

VIETNAM

1959-75
USA
Australia
S.Korea
Philippines
Thailand

1945-54
France
UK

1978▲

1975-78

1965▶

1979
N.Vietnam

1980

KAMPUCHEA

1978-79

1975-77

CHINA

1979

1948▲

1945-54
France
N.Vietnam

1981?(?)

LAOS

1946
1982

1982

(Vietnam-
Thailand)

THAILAND

1982

1954
France

1970-75
USA
N Vietnam

BURMA

1945-48
UK

11
38

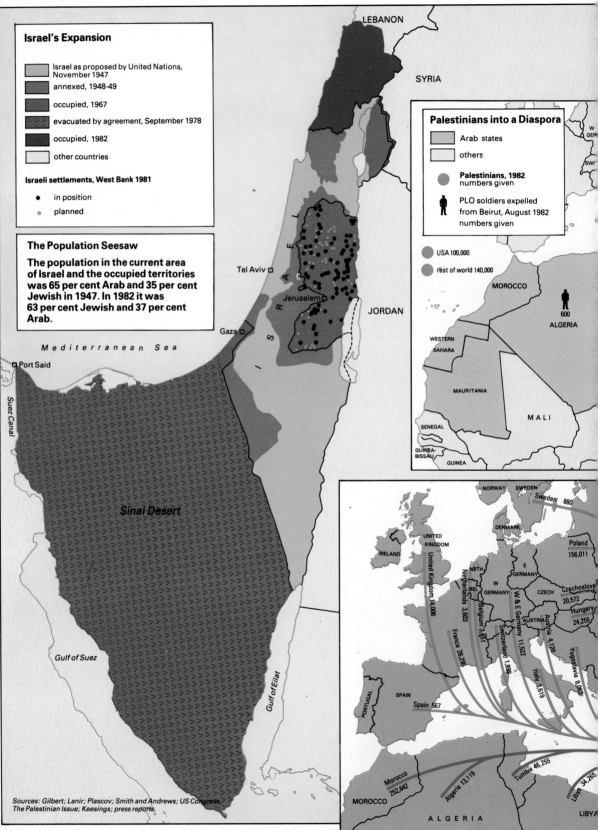

Israel's Expansion

- Israel as proposed by United Nations, November 1947
- annexed, 1948-49
- occupied, 1967
- evacuated by agreement, September 1978
- occupied, 1982
- other countries

Israeli settlements, West Bank 1981

- ● in position
- · planned

The Population Seesaw

The population in the current area of Israel and the occupied territories was 65 per cent Arab and 35 per cent Jewish in 1947. In 1982 it was 63 per cent Jewish and 37 per cent Arab.

Palestinians into a Diaspora

- Arab states
- others
- ● Palestinians, 1982 numbers given
- PLO soldiers expelled from Beirut, August 1982 numbers given

● USA 100,000

● rest of world 140,000

LEBANON

SYRIA

W GER

SWI

Tel Aviv □

Jerusalem □

Gaza □

JORDAN

MOROCCO

WESTERN SAHARA

ALGERIA
600

MAURITANIA

MALI

SENEGAL

GUINEA-BISSAU

GUINEA

Mediterranean Sea

□ Port Said

Suez Canal

Sinai Desert

Gulf of Suez

Gulf of Eilat

ISRAEL

NORWAY SWEDEN
Sweden 880

DENMARK

UNITED KINGDOM

IRELAND

Poland
156,011

NETH
BEL
W GERMANY
E GERMANY
CZECH
Czechoslovakia
20,572

United Kingdom 14,006

Netherlands 3,603

Belgium 3,451

W & E Germany 11,522

AUSTRIA
Austria 4,120

Hungary
24,255

France 26,296

Switzerland 1,899

Italy 3,619

Yugoslavia 8,063

PORTUGAL

SPAIN

Spain 567

Morocco
252,542

Algeria 13,119

Tunisia 46,255

Libya 34,265

MOROCCO

ALGERIA

LIBYA

Sources: Gilbert; Lanir; Plascov; Smith and Andrews; US Congress, The Palestinian Issue; Keesings; press reports.

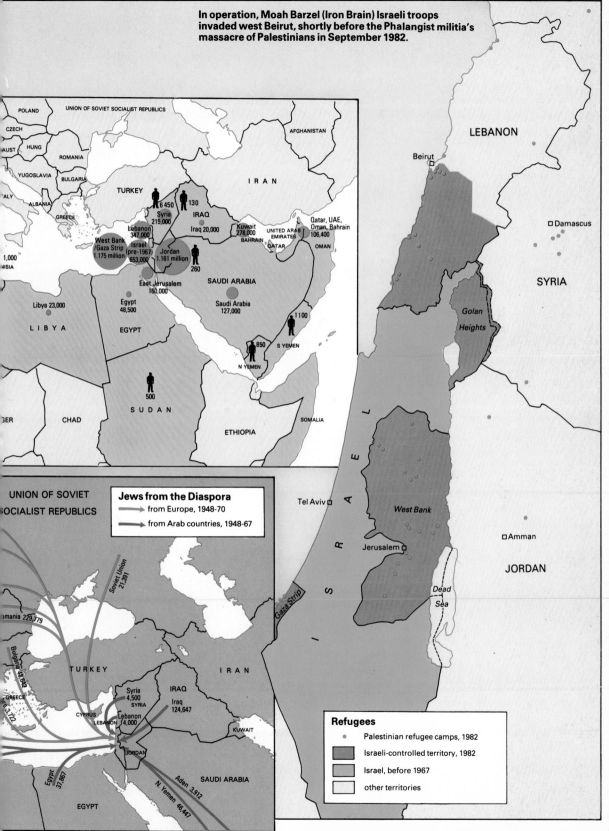

In operation, Moah Barzel (Iron Brain) Israeli troops
invaded west Beirut, shortly before the Phalangist militia's
massacre of Palestinians in September 1982.

LEBANON

Beirut

POLAND

CZECH

AUST — HUNG

YUGOSLAVIA

ALBANIA

ROMANIA

BULGARIA

GREECE

ITALY

UNION OF SOVIET SOCIALIST REPUBLICS

AFGHANISTAN

TURKEY

I R A N

6 450   130

Syria
215,000

IRAQ

Iraq 20,000

Kuwait
278,000

Qatar, UAE,
Oman, Bahrain
106,400

Lebanon
347,000

BAHRAIN

UNITED ARAB
EMIRATES

West Bank
/Gaza Strip
1.175 million

Israel
(pre-1967)
653,000

QATAR

OMAN

Jordan
1.161 million

260

1,000

TUNISIA

East Jerusalem
160,000

SAUDI ARABIA

Libya 23,000

Egypt
48,500

Saudi Arabia
127,000

1100

L I B Y A

EGYPT

S YEMEN

850

N YEMEN

NIGER

CHAD

500

S U D A N

SOMALIA

ETHIOPIA

Damascus

SYRIA

Golan
Heights

Jews from the Diaspora

UNION OF SOVIET
SOCIALIST REPUBLICS

→ from Europe, 1948-70
→ from Arab countries, 1948-67

Soviet Union
21,391

Romania 229,779

Bulgaria 48,692

TURKEY

I R A N

Syria
4,500

IRAQ

Iraq
124,647

SYRIA

CYPRUS

Greece 3,721

LEBANON

Lebanon
14,000

KUWAIT

JORDAN

Egypt
37,857

Aden 3,912

N. Yemen 46,447

SAUDI ARABIA

EGYPT

Tel Aviv

West Bank

Jerusalem

Amman

JORDAN

Dead
Sea

Gaza Strip

I S R A E L

Refugees

- Palestinian refugee camps, 1982
- Israeli-controlled territory, 1982
- Israel, before 1967
- other territories

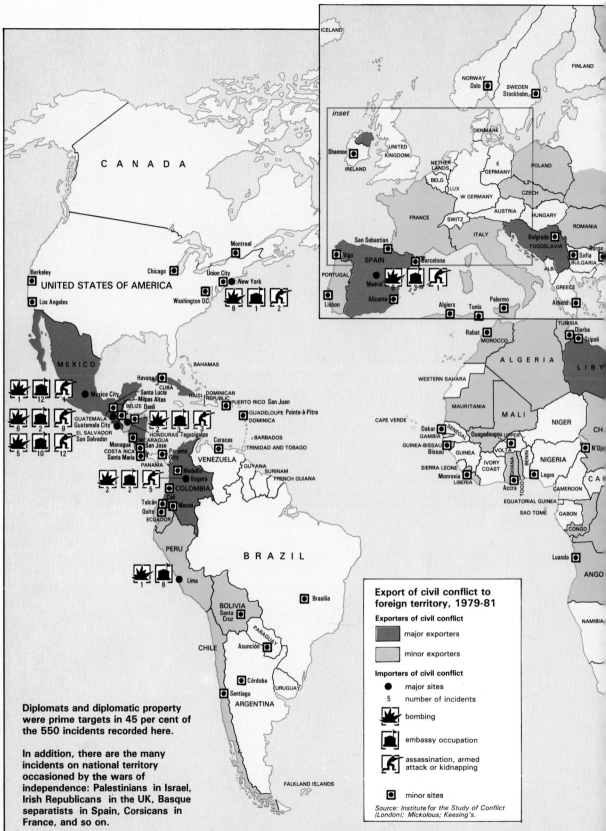

Export of civil conflict to foreign territory, 1979-81

Exporters of civil conflict

- major exporters
- minor exporters

Importers of civil conflict

- ● major sites
- 5 number of incidents
- bombing
- embassy occupation
- assassination, armed attack or kidnapping
- ◉ minor sites

Source: Institute for the Study of Conflict (London); Mickolous; Keesing's.

Diplomats and diplomatic property were prime targets in 45 per cent of the 550 incidents recorded here.

In addition, there are the many incidents on national territory occasioned by the wars of independence: Palestinians in Israel, Irish Republicans in the UK, Basque separatists in Spain, Corsicans in France, and so on.

© Copyright Pluto Press 1983

Cheap transport and instant communication enable domestic enemies to damage their opponents or gain spectacular publicity abroad. In an ordinary week three such incidents occur.

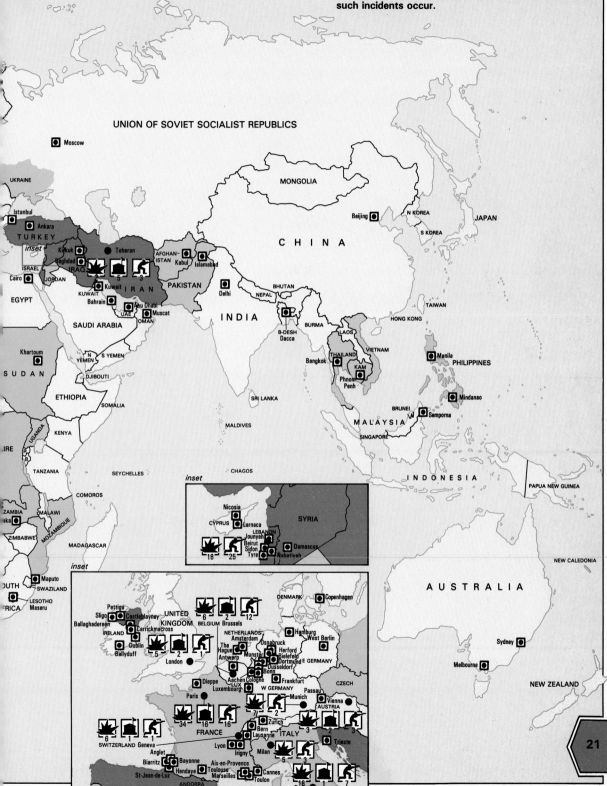

UNION OF SOVIET SOCIALIST REPUBLICS

Moscow

UKRAINE

MONGOLIA

Beijing

N KOREA

S KOREA

JAPAN

CHINA

Istanbul

Ankara

TURKEY

inset

Kirkuk

Baghdad

IRAQ

Teheran

AFGHAN-
ISTAN

Kabul

Islamabad

ISRAEL

Cairo

JORDAN

KUWAIT

Kuwait

IRAN

PAKISTAN

Delhi

TAIWAN

HONG KONG

EGYPT

Bahrain

SAUDI ARABIA

Abu Dhabi

UAE

Muscat

OMAN

INDIA

NEPAL

BHUTAN

BURMA

B-DESH
Dacca

LAOS

VIETNAM

Khartoum

N
YEMEN

S YEMEN

DJIBOUTI

SUDAN

ETHIOPIA

SOMALIA

SRI LANKA

THAILAND

Bangkok

KAM

Phnom
Penh

Manila

PHILIPPINES

Mindanao

MALDIVES

BRUNEI

Semporna

MALAYSIA

SINGAPORE

UGANDA

KENYA

SEYCHELLES

CHAGOS

INDONESIA

PAPUA NEW GUINEA

TANZANIA

COMOROS

ZAMBIA

MALAWI

MADAGASCAR

ZIMBABWE

MOZAMBIQUE

NEW CALEDONIA

Maputo

SWAZILAND

AUSTRALIA

LESOTHO
Maseru

Sydney

Melbourne

NEW ZEALAND

inset

Nicosia

CYPRUS

Larnaca

SYRIA

LEBANON
Jounyeh
Beirut
Sidon
Tyre

Damascus

Nabatiyeh

18   25

inset

Pettigo

Sligo

Castleblayney

UNITED
KINGDOM

6   2   12

BELGIUM Brussels

DENMARK

Copenhagen

Ballaghadereen

Carrickmacross

IRELAND

Dublin

Ballyduff

5   2   1

London

NETHERLANDS
Amsterdam

The
Hague

Antwerp

Osnabruck

Munster

Hamburg

West Berlin

Herford
Bielefeld

E GERMANY

Dieppe

Aachen Cologne

Dortmund
Dusseldorf
Bonn

Frankfurt

CZECH

Paris

LUX
Luxembourg

W GERMANY

Passau

Munich

Vienna

AUSTRIA

7   2

34   16   16

FRANCE

Bern
Lausanne

Zurich

ITALY

3   3

Trieste

6   1

SWITZERLAND Geneva

Lyon

Irigny

Milan

5   3

Anglet

Biarritz

Bayonne

Hendaye

St-Jean-de-Luz

Aix-en-Provence
Toulouse
Marseilles

Cannes

Toulon

18   1   7

ANDORRA

Rome

21

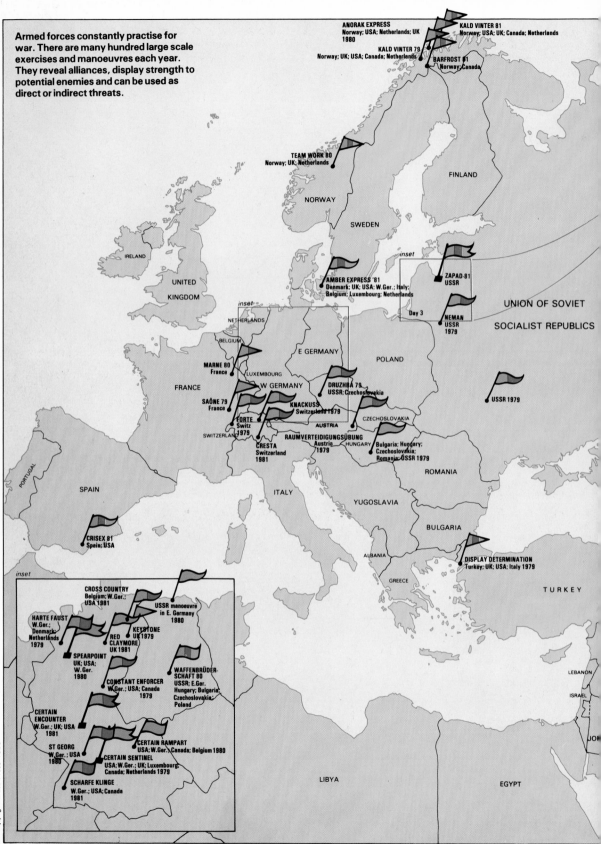

Armed forces constantly practise for war. There are many hundred large scale exercises and manoeuvres each year. They reveal alliances, display strength to potential enemies and can be used as direct or indirect threats.

ANORAK EXPRESS
Norway; USA; Netherlands; UK
1980

KALD VINTER 81
Norway; USA; UK; Canada; Netherlands

KALD VINTER 79
Norway; UK; USA; Canada; Netherlands

BARFROST 81
Norway; Canada

TEAM WORK 80
Norway; UK; Netherlands

FINLAND

NORWAY

SWEDEN

IRELAND

UNITED KINGDOM

inset

ZAPAD-81
USSR

AMBER EXPRESS '81
Denmark; UK; USA; W.Ger.; Italy;
Belgium; Luxembourg; Netherlands

Day 3

NEMAN
USSR
1979

UNION OF SOVIET

SOCIALIST REPUBLICS

NETHERLANDS

BELGIUM

E GERMANY

POLAND

MARNE 80
France

LUXEMBOURG

W GERMANY

DRUZHBA 79
USSR; Czechoslovakia

USSR 1979

SAÔNE 79
France

FRANCE

KNACKUSS
Switzerland 1979

FORTE
Switz
1979

CZECHOSLOVAKIA

SWITZERLAND

CRESTA
Switzerland
1981

RAUMVERTEIDIGUNGSÜBUNG
Austria
1979

AUSTRIA

HUNGARY

Bulgaria; Hungary;
Czechoslovakia;
Romania; USSR 1979

ROMANIA

PORTUGAL

SPAIN

ITALY

YUGOSLAVIA

BULGARIA

CRISEX 81
Spain; USA

ALBANIA

GREECE

DISPLAY DETERMINATION
Turkey; UK; USA; Italy 1979

TURKEY

LEBANON

ISRAEL

JO

inset

CROSS COUNTRY
Belgium; W.Ger.;
USA 1981

USSR manoeuvre
in E. Germany
1980

HARTE FAUST
W.Ger.;
Denmark;
Netherlands
1979

KEYSTONE
UK 1979

RED
CLAYMORE
UK 1981

SPEARPOINT
UK; USA;
W.Ger.
1980

WAFFENBRÜDER-
SCHAFT 80
USSR; E.Ger.
Hungary; Bulgaria;
Czechoslovakia;
Poland

CONSTANT ENFORCER
W.Ger.; USA; Canada
1979

CERTAIN
ENCOUNTER
W.Ger.; UK; USA
1981

ST GEORG
W.Ger.; USA
1980

CERTAIN RAMPART
USA; W.Ger.; Canada; Belgium 1980

CERTAIN SENTINEL
USA; W.Ger.; UK; Luxembourg;
Canada; Netherlands 1979

SCHARFE KLINGE
W.Ger.; USA; Canada
1981

LIBYA

EGYPT

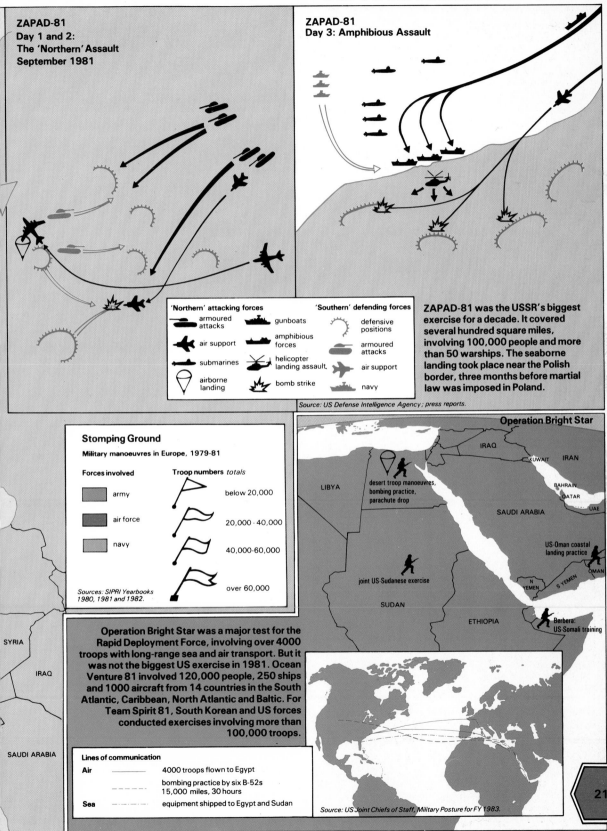

ZAPAD-81
Day 1 and 2:
The 'Northern' Assault
September 1981

ZAPAD-81
Day 3: Amphibious Assault

'Northern' attacking forces

- armoured attacks
- air support
- submarines
- airborne landing
- gunboats
- amphibious forces
- helicopter landing assault
- bomb strike

'Southern' defending forces

- defensive positions
- armoured attacks
- air support
- navy

ZAPAD-81 was the USSR's biggest exercise for a decade. It covered several hundred square miles, involving 100,000 people and more than 50 warships. The seaborne landing took place near the Polish border, three months before martial law was imposed in Poland.

Source: US Defense Intelligence Agency ; press reports.

Stomping Ground

Military manoeuvres in Europe, 1979-81

Forces involved

- army
- air force
- navy

Troop numbers *totals*

- below 20,000
- 20,000 - 40,000
- 40,000-60,000
- over 60,000

Sources: SIPRI Yearbooks
1980, 1981 and 1982.

Operation Bright Star

IRAQ
KUWAIT
IRAN
BAHRAIN
QATAR
UAE
LIBYA
desert troop manoeuvres, bombing practice, parachute drop
SAUDI ARABIA
US-Oman coastal landing practice
joint US-Sudanese exercise
N YEMEN
S YEMEN
OMAN
SUDAN
ETHIOPIA
Berbera: US-Somali training

SYRIA
IRAQ
SAUDI ARABIA

Operation Bright Star was a major test for the Rapid Deployment Force, involving over 4000 troops with long-range sea and air transport. But it was not the biggest US exercise in 1981. Ocean Venture 81 involved 120,000 people, 250 ships and 1000 aircraft from 14 countries in the South Atlantic, Caribbean, North Atlantic and Baltic. For Team Spirit 81, South Korean and US forces conducted exercises involving more than 100,000 troops.

Lines of communication

Air		4000 troops flown to Egypt
		bombing practice by six B-52s 15,000 miles, 30 hours
Sea		equipment shipped to Egypt and Sudan

Source: US Joint Chiefs of Staff, Military Posture for FY 1983.

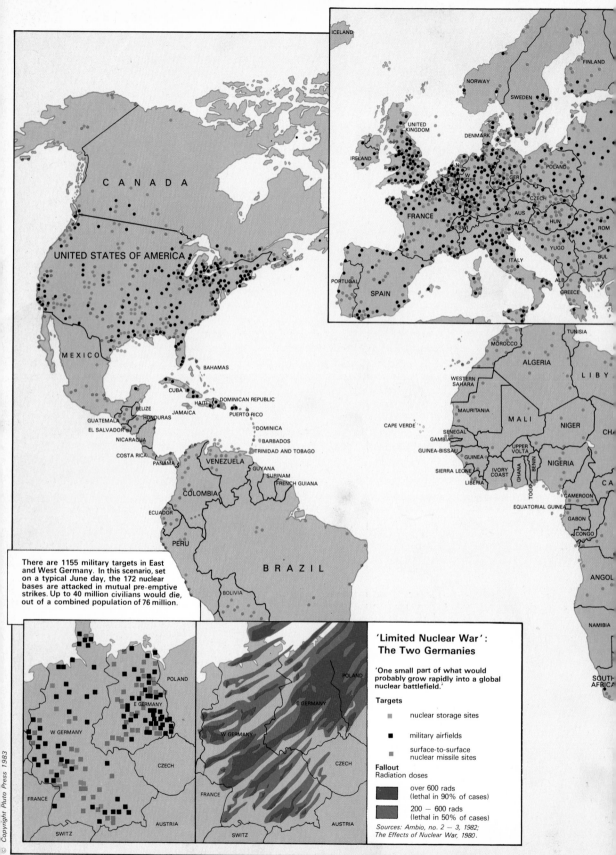

There are 1155 military targets in East and West Germany. In this scenario, set on a typical June day, the 172 nuclear bases are attacked in mutual pre-emptive strikes. Up to 40 million civilians would die, out of a combined population of 76 million.

'Limited Nuclear War': The Two Germanies

'One small part of what would probably grow rapidly into a global nuclear battlefield.'

Targets

- nuclear storage sites
- military airfields
- surface-to-surface nuclear missile sites

Fallout
Radiation doses

- over 600 rads (lethal in 90% of cases)
- 200 — 600 rads (lethal in 50% of cases)

Sources: Ambio, no. 2 – 3, 1982; The Effects of Nuclear War, 1980.

The USA's strategic plan designates 40,000 targets world-wide, including 60 within Moscow alone. The number of targets for Soviet weapons is unknown.

UNION OF SOVIET SOCIALIST REPUBLICS

MONGOLIA

JAPAN

N KOREA

S KOREA

CHINA

TURKEY

LEBANON
SYRIA
ISRAEL JOR
IRAQ
IRAN
AFGHANISTAN

TAIWAN

KUWAIT

BAHRAIN QATAR
UAE
SAUDI ARABIA
OMAN
PAKISTAN
NEPAL
BHUTAN
BURMA
HONG KONG

EGYPT

B-DESH
LAOS
VIETNAM

SUDAN
N YEMEN
S YEMEN

INDIA

THAILAND
KAM

DJIBOUTI

ETHIOPIA
SOMALIA

SRI LANKA

PHILIPPINES

UGANDA
KENYA

AIRE

BRUNEI

MALAYSIA

SINGAPORE

TANZANIA

COMOROS

INDONESIA

ZAMBIA
MALAWI

PAPUA NEW GUINEA

ZIMBABWE
MOZAMBIQUE
MADAGASCAR

We do not know how nuclear war would be waged. In this scenario, 14,747 nuclear warheads are detonated, less than half the explosive power of the USA and USSR.

Of the 1300 million urban population in the northern hemisphere, 750 million would die immediately. 340 million would be seriously injured. Additional deaths through heat and fire are incalculable.

AUSTRALIA

Immediately following the war, rainwater would be a deadly poison. Contamination of freshwater reservoirs would last for several years. Agriculture would be ruined and industrialised societies crippled. One-third of survivors would suffer severe psychiatric disorders. Energy, distribution of food, communications, sanitation and health systems would break down.

NEW ZEALAND

North of the tropics, a small fraction of survivors would escape disease and famine in the following year. Poor countries, dependent on outside supplies of food and technology might be worst affected. Deaths in them could exceed 2 billion.

Major strategic nuclear target areas

- urban targets
- military targets
- energy targets outside other areas

Source: Ambio, no. 2 – 3, 1982.

9
17
19

Part Two: Weaponry

The USA and the USSR are unmatched in their acquisition of
the hardware of war. Not only do they command the full panoply
of modern weapons, they define its extent. They set the
standards and the fashion for states lower down the hierarchy.
Immediately below them are states possessing a wide range of
the most sophisticated conventional weapons, some of them
members of the nuclear club. Below them, following the fashion
begins to fade into imitation, with each state buying something
of almost everything. At the bottom, the poorest and weakest

purchase a little of something, sometimes for use, often for appearances.

Within this global hierarchy, there is a series of local and regional ones. It can be exemplified by Uruguay and Paraguay between Argentina and Brazil, or by the disparities of power in Southern Africa.

Yet the hierarchies are not stable. If anything should alert us to the dangers of nuclear proliferation and the weakness of the safeguards against it, it is the Israeli bombing raid in September 1980 on Osiraq, the Iraqi nuclear reactor. Although Iraq is a party to the Nuclear Non-Proliferation Treaty, it was suspected by Israel, a non-party, of preparing to evade the treaty's provisions by proceeding from nuclear research to the manufacture of nuclear weapons (see the inset to *Map 10: Insecurity in Numbers*).

These dangers will remain as long as nuclear-armed states retain their nuclear arsenals. Israel and South Africa are suspected of already having nuclear weapons. India conducted a nuclear test in 1974. Along with the majority of states, the superpowers have acknowledged the dangers in the spread of nuclear weapons by supporting the Nuclear Non-Proliferation Treaty. But they oppose nuclear proliferation as much because of its threat to their power as because of its threat to life. They have not merely retained their nuclear arsenals, they have increased and modernised them. Britain and France even argue that they should retain nuclear weapons to guard against the threats which will be produced by the very nuclear proliferation their examples encourage.

Another of the darker sides of the international military order is the existence of chemical and biological weapons (see *Map 11: Bugs and Poisons*). These weapons provoke deeply fearful reactions. As a result, their use has been alleged far more often than has been admitted, and they have been restricted by international treaties. The 1925 Geneva Convention outlawed their use, except as retaliation in kind, and the production of biological weapons has been forbidden by the Biological Warfare Convention since 1975. The latter is the only treaty of actual disarmament agreed since 1945. Despite these agreements, it is clear that the science and technology of these weapons are available. How widely available is not known.

The advance of military technology has opened frontiers which until recently only fantasists crossed. On a clear, summer night you can lie on your back out of doors and see several small coloured lights moving across the sky. They are satellites. About three-quarters of them are military and their functions are increasingly important to the superpowers' military machines (see *Map 12: Star Wars*). Not the least crucial part of a war between the USA and USSR would be the war in outer space.

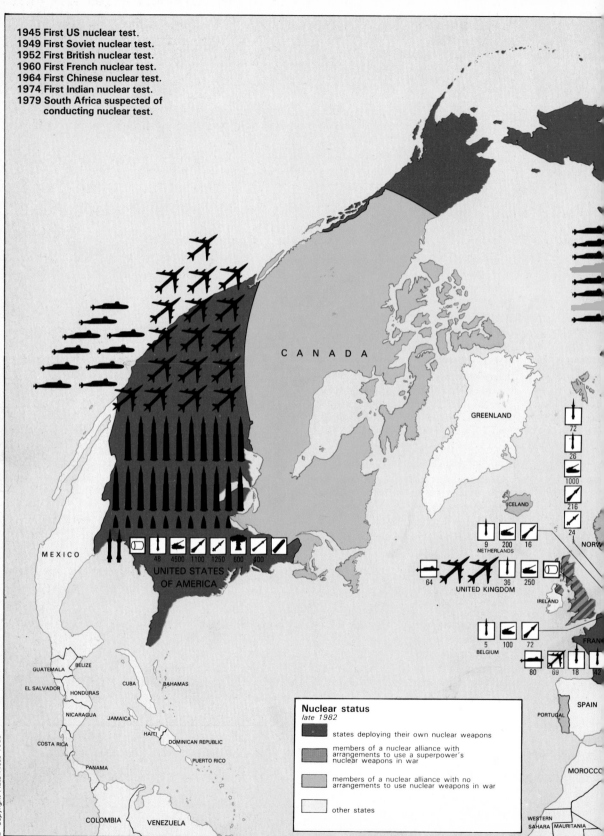

1945 First US nuclear test.
1949 First Soviet nuclear test.
1952 First British nuclear test.
1960 First French nuclear test.
1964 First Chinese nuclear test.
1974 First Indian nuclear test.
1979 South Africa suspected of
conducting nuclear test.

C A N A D A

GREENLAND

ICELAND

72

26

1000

216

24

9   200   16
NETHERLANDS

NOR

MEXICO

48   4500 1100 1250   600   400

UNITED STATES
OF AMERICA

64   36   250
        UNITED KINGDOM

IRELAND

FRAN

5   100   72
BELGIUM

80   69   18   42

GUATEMALA   BELIZE

EL SALVADOR   CUBA   BAHAMAS

HONDURAS

NICARAGUA   JAMAICA

COSTA RICA   HAITI
        DOMINICAN REPUBLIC

PUERTO RICO

PANAMA

SPAIN

PORTUGAL

MOROCCO

COLOMBIA   VENEZUELA

WESTERN
SAHARA   MAURITANIA

Nuclear status
late 1982

states deploying their own nuclear weapons

members of a nuclear alliance with
arrangements to use a superpower's
nuclear weapons in war

members of a nuclear alliance with no
arrangements to use nuclear weapons in war

other states

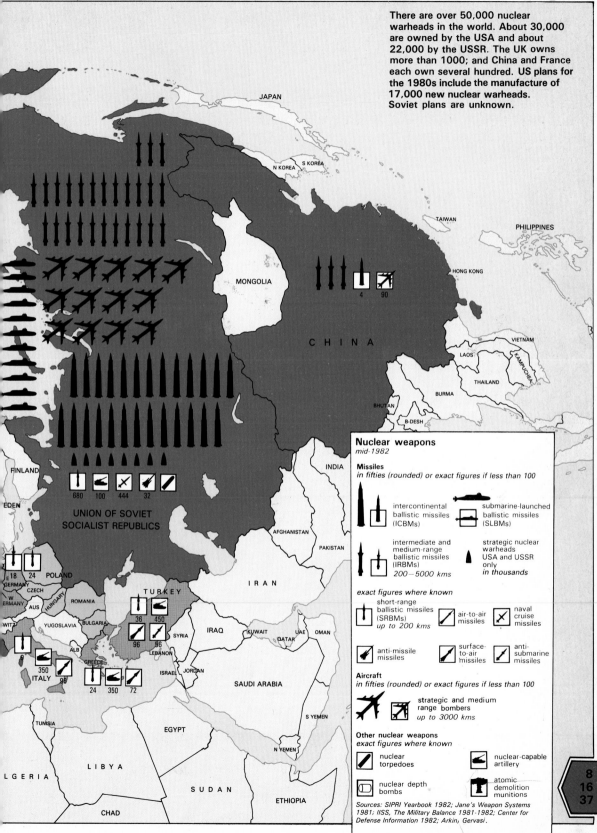

There are over 50,000 nuclear warheads in the world. About 30,000 are owned by the USA and about 22,000 by the USSR. The UK owns more than 1000; and China and France each own several hundred. US plans for the 1980s include the manufacture of 17,000 new nuclear warheads. Soviet plans are unknown.

JAPAN

N KOREA   S KOREA

TAIWAN

PHILIPPINES

MONGOLIA

HONG KONG

C H I N A

VIETNAM

LAOS

KAMPUCHEA

THAILAND

BURMA

BHUTAN

B-DESH

4   90

FINLAND

INDIA

AFGHANISTAN

PAKISTAN

EDEN

680   100   444   32

UNION OF SOVIET
SOCIALIST REPUBLICS

E 18   24   POLAND

GERMANY
CZECH

W
ERMANY

AUS   HUNGARY

ROMANIA

WITZ   YUGOSLAVIA   BULGARIA

T U R K E Y

I R A N

ALB

36   450

9

96   56

SYRIA   IRAQ   KUWAIT   UAE   OMAN
LEBANON   QATAR

350   GREECE

96   ISRAEL   JORDAN

ITALY

24   350   72

SAUDI ARABIA

S YEMEN

TUNISIA

EGYPT

N YEMEN

LGERIA

L I B Y A

SUDAN

CHAD

ETHIOPIA

Nuclear weapons
mid-1982

Missiles
in fifties (rounded) or exact figures if less than 100

intercontinental ballistic missiles (ICBMs)

submarine-launched ballistic missiles (SLBMs)

intermediate and medium-range ballistic missiles (IRBMs) 200—5000 kms

strategic nuclear warheads USA and USSR only *in thousands*

exact figures where known

short-range ballistic missiles (SRBMs) *up to 200 kms*

air-to-air missiles

naval cruise missiles

anti-missile missiles

surface-to-air missiles

anti-submarine missiles

Aircraft
in fifties (rounded) or exact figures if less than 100

strategic and medium range bombers *up to 3000 kms*

Other nuclear weapons
exact figures where known

nuclear torpedoes

nuclear-capable artillery

nuclear depth bombs

atomic demolition munitions

8
16
37

Sources: SIPRI Yearbook 1982; Jane's Weapon Systems 1981; IISS, The Military Balance 1981-1982; Center for Defense Information 1982; Arkin, Gervasi.

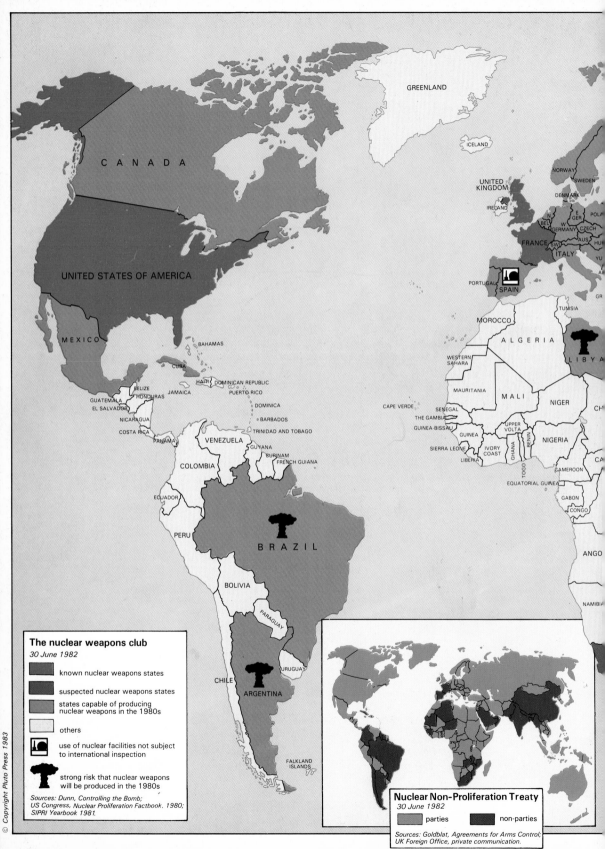

The nuclear weapons club
30 June 1982

known nuclear weapons states

suspected nuclear weapons states

states capable of producing
nuclear weapons in the 1980s

others

use of nuclear facilities not subject
to international inspection

strong risk that nuclear weapons
will be produced in the 1980s

Sources: Dunn, Controlling the Bomb;
US Congress, Nuclear Proliferation Factbook. 1980;
SIPRI Yearbook 1981.

Nuclear Non-Proliferation Treaty
30 June 1982

parties   non-parties

Sources: Goldblat, Agreements for Arms Control;
UK Foreign Office, private communication.

10. Insecurity in Numbers

The USA's original nuclear monopoly was broken by the USSR. The duopoly was broken by the UK. The oligopoly was extended by France and China, then India, and probably Israel and South Africa. There are many preparing to join the club.

UNION OF SOVIET SOCIALIST REPUBLICS

MONGOLIA

TURKEY
SYRIA
LEBANON
ISRAEL
JORDAN
IRAQ
KUWAIT
I R A N
AFGHANISTAN
PAKISTAN
NEPAL
BHUTAN
B'DESH
C H I N A
N KOREA
S KOREA
JAPAN
S KOREA
TAIWAN

UAE
EGYPT
SAUDI ARABIA
OMAN
INDIA
BURMA
LAOS
VIETNAM
PHILIPPINES

N YEMEN
S YEMEN
DJIBOUTI
SUDAN
ETHIOPIA
SOMALIA
THAILAND
KAM
BRUNEI
SRI LANKA
MALAYSIA

UGANDA
KENYA
AIRE
TANZANIA
COMOROS
INDONESIA
PAPUA NEW GUINEA

ZAMBIA
MALAWI
ZIMBABWE
MOZAMBIQUE
MADAGASCAR

India has detonated a nuclear explosive and therefore qualifies as a nuclear weapons state, even though there is no evidence so far that it has deployed nuclear weapons.

A U S T R A L I A

NEW ZEALAND

Nuclear Friends and Foes
Iraq's nuclear reactor at Osiraq

Paris
ISRAEL assassinates Egyptian metallurgist Yihya al-Meshad, a 'pillar of Iraq's nuclear program' 13 June 1980

FRANCE

Toulon
ISRAEL sabotages reactor core en route to Iraq, 9 April 1979

reactor from FRANCE
'hot cell' from ITALY
Osiraq
IRAQ
technical aid from BRAZIL
uranium from PORTUGAL, NIGER, BRAZIL

IRAN bombs and damages Osiraq 30 September 1980
ISRAEL bombs and destroys Osiraq reactor 7 June 1981

IRAQ

Sources: Feldman, The Raid on Osiraq; US Congress, Israeli attack on Iraqi Nuclear Facilities.

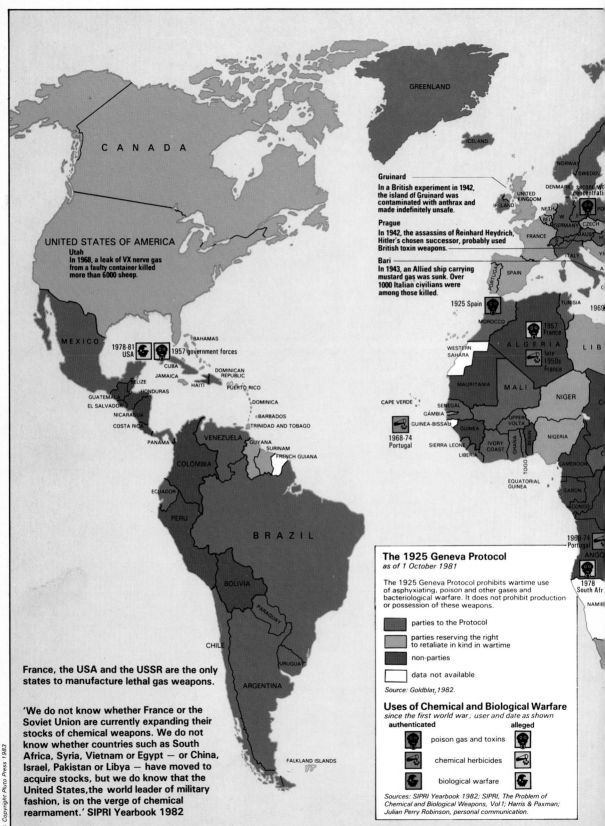

GREENLAND

ICELAND

Gruinard

In a British experiment in 1942, the island of Gruinard was contaminated with anthrax and made indefinitely unsafe.

Prague

In 1942, the assassins of Reinhard Heydrich, Hitler's chosen successor, probably used British toxin weapons.

Bari

In 1943, an Allied ship carrying mustard gas was sunk. Over 1000 Italian civilians were among those killed.

C A N A D A

UNITED KINGDOM

IRELAND

NETH.

BEL.

W. GERMANY

DENMARK

NORWAY

SWEDEN

second w concentrati

PO

CZECH

FRANCE

AUS

H

ITALY

Y

SPAIN

PORTUGAL

A

1925 Spain

TUNISIA

1969

UNITED STATES OF AMERICA

Utah

In 1968, a leak of VX nerve gas from a faulty container killed more than 6000 sheep.

MOROCCO

1957 France

A L G E R I A

L I B

M E X I C O

1978-81 USA

1957 government forces

WESTERN SAHARA

late 1950s France

BAHAMAS

CUBA

DOMINICAN REPUBLIC

JAMAICA

HAITI

PUERTO RICO

DOMINICA

BARBADOS

TRINIDAD AND TOBAGO

MAURITANIA

M A L I

NIGER

BELIZE

HONDURAS

GUATEMALA

EL SALVADOR

NICARAGUA

COSTA RICA

PANAMA

VENEZUELA

GUYANA

SURINAM

FRENCH GUIANA

COLOMBIA

ECUADOR

CAPE VERDE

SENEGAL

GAMBIA

GUINEA-BISSAU

1968-74 Portugal

GUINEA

SIERRA LEONE

LIBERIA

IVORY COAST

GHANA

TOGO

BENIN

NIGERIA

CAMEROON

EQUATORIAL GUINEA

GABON

CONGO

UPPER VOLTA

PERU

B R A Z I L

BOLIVIA

PARAGUAY

CHILE

URUGUAY

ARGENTINA

FALKLAND ISLANDS

1968-74 Portugal

ANGO

1978 South Afr

NAMIB

France, the USA and the USSR are the only states to manufacture lethal gas weapons.

'We do not know whether France or the Soviet Union are currently expanding their stocks of chemical weapons. We do not know whether countries such as South Africa, Syria, Vietnam or Egypt — or China, Israel, Pakistan or Libya — have moved to acquire stocks, but we do know that the United States, the world leader of military fashion, is on the verge of chemical rearmament.' SIPRI Yearbook 1982

The 1925 Geneva Protocol
as of 1 October 1981

The 1925 Geneva Protocol prohibits wartime use of asphyxiating, poison and other gases and bacteriological warfare. It does not prohibit production or possession of these weapons.

	parties to the Protocol
	parties reserving the right to retaliate in kind in wartime
	non-parties
	data not available

Source: Goldblat, 1982.

Uses of Chemical and Biological Warfare
since the first world war; user and date as shown

authenticated		alleged
	poison gas and toxins	
	chemical herbicides	
	biological warfare	

Sources: SIPRI Yearbook 1982; SIPRI, The Problem of Chemical and Biological Weapons, Vol 1; Harris & Paxman; Julian Perry Robinson, personal communication.

11. Bugs and Poisons

It needs a single droplet of nerve gas on the skin to kill. The US stockpile of nerve gas contains enough lethal doses to kill the world's population some 4000 times.

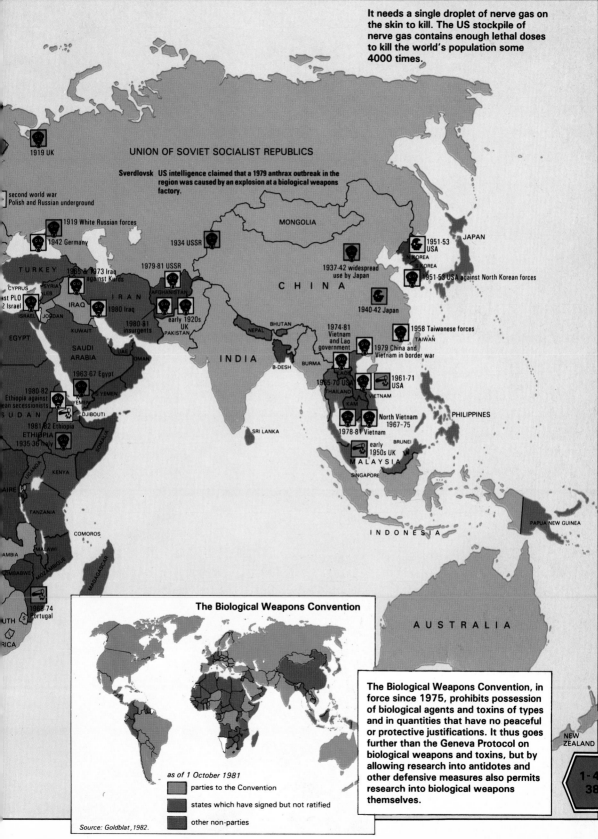

1919 UK

UNION OF SOVIET SOCIALIST REPUBLICS

Sverdlovsk US intelligence claimed that a 1979 anthrax outbreak in the region was caused by an explosion at a biological weapons factory.

second world war Polish and Russian underground

1919 White Russian forces

1942 Germany

1934 USSR

MONGOLIA

JAPAN

1951-53 USA
N KOREA
S KOREA

1951-53 USA against North Korean forces

TURKEY

1965 & 1973 Iraq against Kurds

1979-81 USSR

CYPRUS
SYRIA
LEB
st PLO
2 Israel
IRAQ
ISRAEL
JORDAN
1980 Iraq
AFGHANISTAN
early 1920s UK
PAKISTAN
1980-81 insurgents

1937-42 widespread use by Japan

CHINA

1940-42 Japan

1958 Taiwanese forces
TAIWAN

1974-81 Vietnam and Lao government

1979 China and Vietnam in border war

EGYPT
KUWAIT
SAUDI ARABIA
UAE
OMAN

INDIA
NEPAL
BHUTAN
B-DESH
BURMA
LAOS
THAILAND
1965-70 USA
KAM
VIETNAM
1961-71 USA

1963-67 Egypt
S.YEMEN
YEMEN
DJIBOUTI

1980-82 Ethiopia against ean secessionists

1981-82 Ethiopia
ETHIOPIA
1935-36 Italy
SOMALIA

SRI LANKA

North Vietnam 1967-75

1978-81 Vietnam

early 1950s UK
MALAYSIA
BRUNEI
SINGAPORE

PHILIPPINES

UGANDA
AIRE
KENYA
TANZANIA
COMOROS

INDONESIA

PAPUA NEW GUINEA

AMBIA
MALAWI
ZIMBABWE
MOZAMBIQUE
MADAGASCAR

1968-74 Portugal
UTH
RICA

AUSTRALIA

The Biological Weapons Convention

as of 1 October 1981

- parties to the Convention
- states which have signed but not ratified
- other non-parties

Source: Goldblat, 1982.

The Biological Weapons Convention, in force since 1975, prohibits possession of biological agents and toxins of types and in quantities that have no peaceful or protective justifications. It thus goes further than the Geneva Protocol on biological weapons and toxins, but by allowing research into antidotes and other defensive measures also permits research into biological weapons themselves.

NEW ZEALAND

1-4
38

'Control of space will be decided in the next decade.
If the Soviets control space, they can control the earth,
as in past centuries the nation that controlled the seas
dominated the continents.'   John F. Kennedy, 1960.

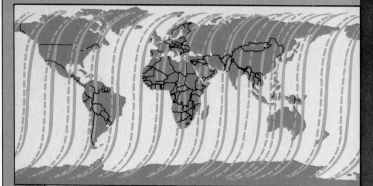

Sinister Footprints
Ground tracks over 24 hours

/ 1980 – 10A   / 1981 – 85A

Two US KH-11 satellites have been in simultaneous orbit virtually
the whole time since 1980. The orbits are spaced to track
different parts of the earth's surface at any one moment and to
fill the gaps between each other's field of observation.

Star Wars

Every ten seconds $4000 are spent on the military uses of outer
space. Every three days a military satellite is launched.
Of 2725 satellites launched between 1957 and 1981, 1917 (70
per cent) were for military purposes. Military satellites are used for
reconnaissance, early warning, communications, navigation and
research, and will be used increasingly for mid-flight guidance for
ballistic missiles. The USSR is deploying anti-satellite satellites
while the USA develops anti-satellite missiles.

The Space Shuttle

In March 1981, NASA, the US National Aeronautics and Space
Administration, launched Orbiter Columbia, the first reusable
space vehicle.
Nine of the 44 missions planned for it up to September 1985 were
wholly booked by the US Department of Defense, which sees it as
a means to:

● place military satellites in orbit more cheaply and efficiently
  than through launches from earth.

● capture, destroy and derange enemy satellites

● carry nuclear weapons virtually immune from attack

● carry people and materials for making weapons such as high-
  power lasers.

shuttle
USA

Sources: Jasani; Financial Times.

ele
US

photographic rec
USA 235; USSR

interception/destru
USSR 33

fractional orbital bombardment syste
USSR 17

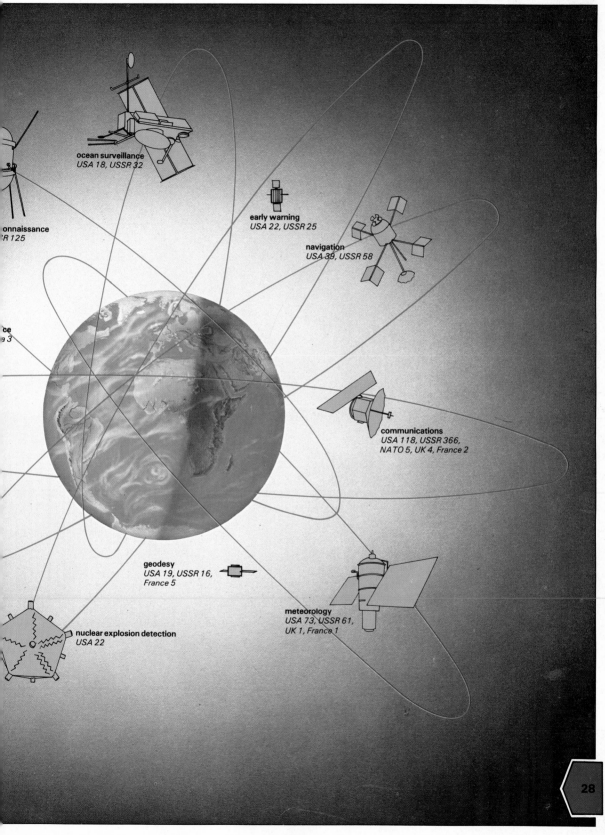

ocean surveillance
USA 18, USSR 32

...onnaissance
...R 125

early warning
USA 22, USSR 25

navigation
USA 39, USSR 58

...ce
...a 3

communications
*USA 118, USSR 366,
NATO 5, UK 4, France 2*

geodesy
*USA 19, USSR 16,
France 5*

meteorology
*USA 73, USSR 61,
UK 1, France 1*

nuclear explosion detection
USA 22

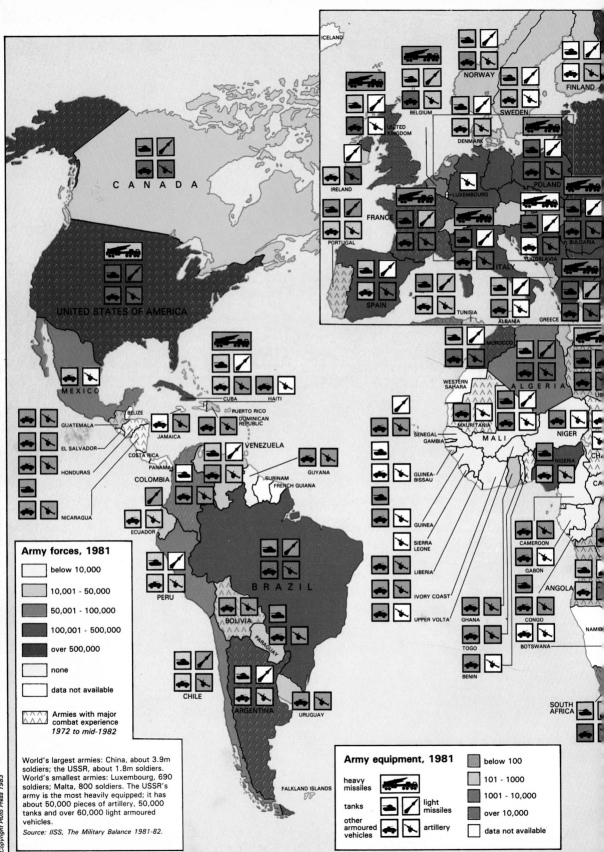

Army forces, 1981

- below 10,000
- 10,001 - 50,000
- 50,001 - 100,000
- 100,001 - 500,000
- over 500,000
- none
- data not available
- Armies with major combat experience 1972 to mid-1982

World's largest armies: China, about 3.9m soldiers; the USSR, about 1.8m soldiers. World's smallest armies: Luxembourg, 690 soldiers; Malta, 800 soldiers. The USSR's army is the most heavily equipped; it has about 50,000 pieces of artillery, 50,000 tanks and over 60,000 light armoured vehicles.

Source: IISS, The Military Balance 1981-82.

Army equipment, 1981

- heavy missiles
- tanks
- other armoured vehicles
- light missiles
- artillery

- below 100
- 101 - 1000
- 1001 - 10,000
- over 10,000
- data not available

CANADA

UNITED STATES OF AMERICA

MEXICO

GUATEMALA
BELIZE
EL SALVADOR
HONDURAS
NICARAGUA
COSTA RICA
PANAMA
JAMAICA
CUBA
HAITI
PUERTO RICO
DOMINICAN REPUBLIC
VENEZUELA
GUYANA
SURINAM
FRENCH GUIANA
COLOMBIA
ECUADOR
PERU
BOLIVIA
BRAZIL
PARAGUAY
CHILE
ARGENTINA
URUGUAY
FALKLAND ISLANDS

ICELAND
IRELAND
UNITED KINGDOM
NORWAY
BELGIUM
DENMARK
SWEDEN
FINLAND
FRANCE
LUXEMBOURG
PORTUGAL
SPAIN
ITALY
POLAND
BULGARIA
YUGOSLAVIA
ALBANIA
GREECE
TUNISIA

MOROCCO
WESTERN SAHARA
ALGERIA
MAURITANIA
MALI
NIGER
SENEGAL
GAMBIA
GUINEA-BISSAU
GUINEA
SIERRA LEONE
LIBERIA
IVORY COAST
UPPER VOLTA
NIGERIA
GHANA
TOGO
BENIN
CAMEROON
GABON
CONGO
ANGOLA
NAMIBIA
BOTSWANA
SOUTH AFRICA

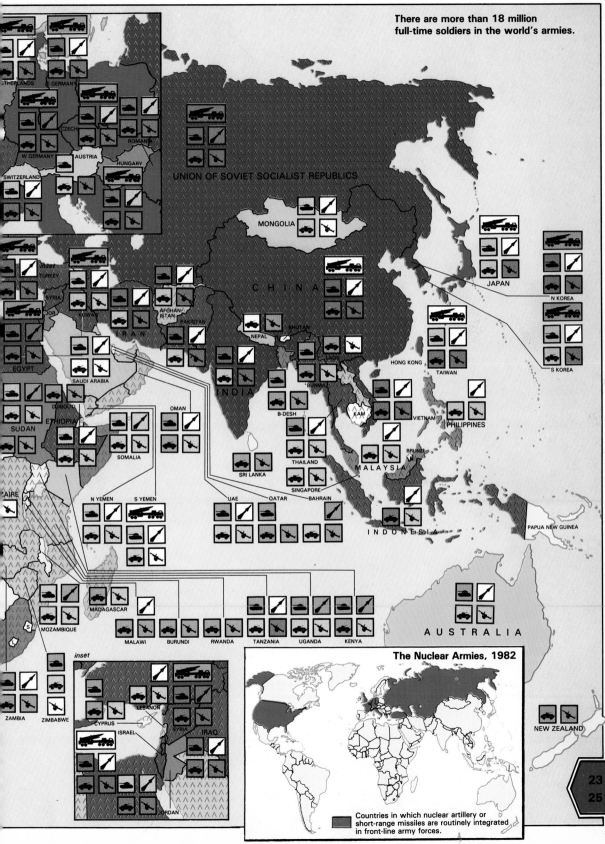

There are more than 18 million
full-time soldiers in the world's armies.

NETHERLANDS
E GERMANY
CZECH
ROMANIA
W GERMANY
AUSTRIA
HUNGARY
SWITZERLAND

UNION OF SOVIET SOCIALIST REPUBLICS

MONGOLIA

JAPAN

N KOREA

S KOREA

inset
TURKEY
SYRIA
JOR
KUWAIT
IRAN
AFGHAN-
ISTAN
PAKISTAN
NEPAL
BHUTAN

C H I N A

HONG KONG

TAIWAN

EGYPT

SAUDI ARABIA

INDIA

B-DESH

BURMA

KAM

VIETNAM

PHILIPPINES

DJIBOUTI

ETHIOPIA

OMAN

SOMALIA

SRI LANKA

THAILAND

BRUNEI

M A L A Y S I A

SUDAN

AIRE

N YEMEN

S YEMEN

UAE

QATAR

BAHRAIN

SINGAPORE

I N D O N E S I A

PAPUA NEW GUINEA

MADAGASCAR

MOZAMBIQUE

MALAWI

BURUNDI

RWANDA

TANZANIA

UGANDA

KENYA

A U S T R A L I A

inset

ZAMBIA

ZIMBABWE

CYPRUS

LEBANON

ISRAEL

SYRIA

IRAQ

JORDAN

NEW ZEALAND

The Nuclear Armies, 1982

Countries in which nuclear artillery or
short-range missiles are routinely integrated
in front-line army forces.

23
25

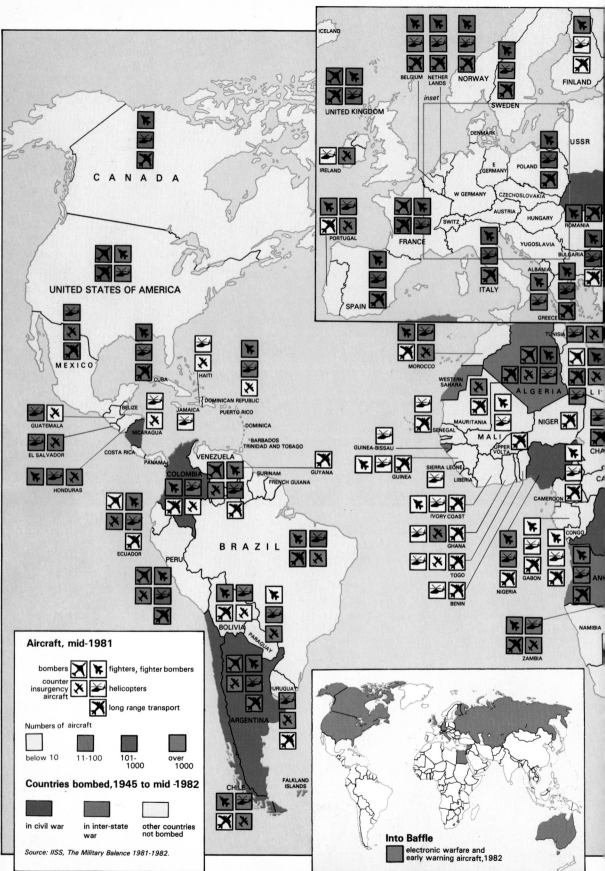

Aircraft, mid-1981

bombers   fighters, fighter bombers

counter insurgency aircraft   helicopters

long range transport

Numbers of aircraft

below 10   11-100   101-1000   over 1000

Countries bombed, 1945 to mid -1982

in civil war   in inter-state war   other countries not bombed

Source: IISS, The Military Balance 1981-1982.

Into Baffle

electronic warfare and early warning aircraft, 1982

14. In the Air

There are about 60,000 combat aircraft in the world's air forces. 60 per cent of them are owned by NATO and Warsaw Pact countries.

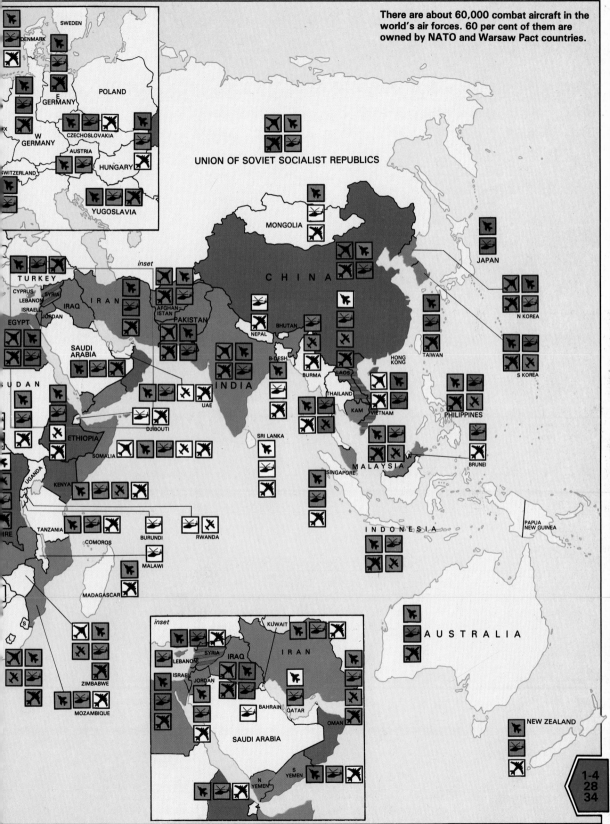

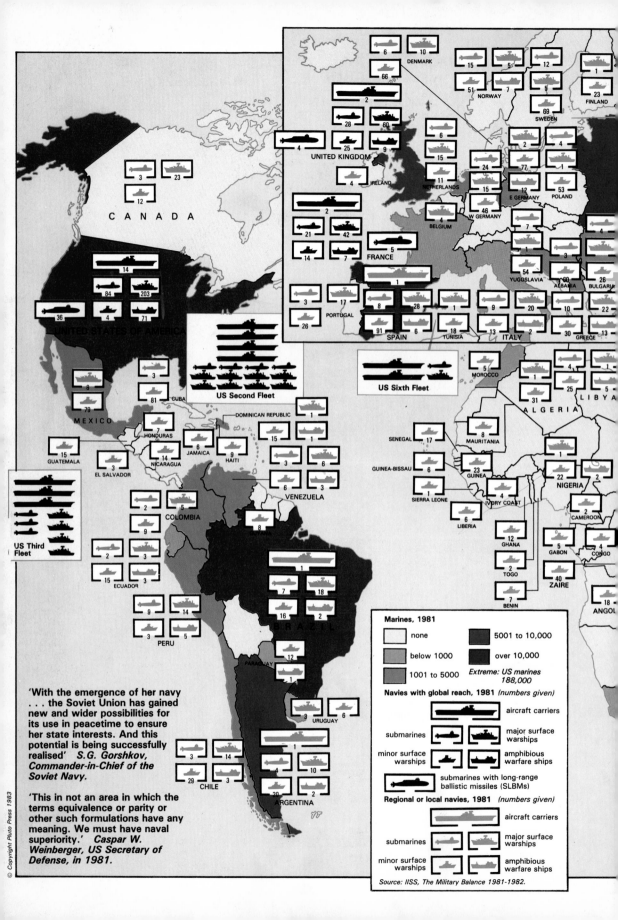

CANADA

UNITED STATES OF AMERICA

US Second Fleet

US Third Fleet

MEXICO

GUATEMALA
EL SALVADOR
HONDURAS
NICARAGUA
CUBA
JAMAICA
HAITI
DOMINICAN REPUBLIC

VENEZUELA

COLOMBIA

GUYANA

ECUADOR

PERU

B R A Z I L

PARAGUAY

URUGUAY

CHILE

ARGENTINA

DENMARK
NORWAY
FINLAND
SWEDEN
UNITED KINGDOM
IRELAND
NETHERLANDS
E GERMANY
POLAND
W GERMANY
BELGIUM
FRANCE
YUGOSLAVIA
ALBANIA
BULGARIA
PORTUGAL
SPAIN
TUNISIA
ITALY
GREECE

US Sixth Fleet

MOROCCO
ALGERIA
LIBYA

SENEGAL
MAURITANIA
GUINEA-BISSAU
GUINEA
SIERRA LEONE
IVORY COAST
LIBERIA
GHANA
NIGERIA
CAMEROON
GABON
CONGO
TOGO
BENIN
ZAIRE
ANGOLA

'With the emergence of her navy . . . the Soviet Union has gained new and wider possibilities for its use in peacetime to ensure her state interests. And this potential is being successfully realised' *S.G. Gorshkov, Commander-in-Chief of the Soviet Navy.*

'This in not an area in which the terms equivalence or parity or other such formulations have any meaning. We must have naval superiority.' *Caspar W. Weinberger, US Secretary of Defense, in 1981.*

Marines, 1981

none
below 1000
1001 to 5000
5001 to 10,000
over 10,000
Extreme: US marines 188,000

Navies with global reach, 1981 *(numbers given)*

aircraft carriers
submarines
major surface warships
minor surface warships
amphibious warfare ships
submarines with long-range ballistic missiles (SLBMs)

Regional or local navies, 1981 *(numbers given)*

aircraft carriers
submarines
major surface warships
minor surface warships
amphibious warfare ships

Source: IISS, The Military Balance 1981-1982.

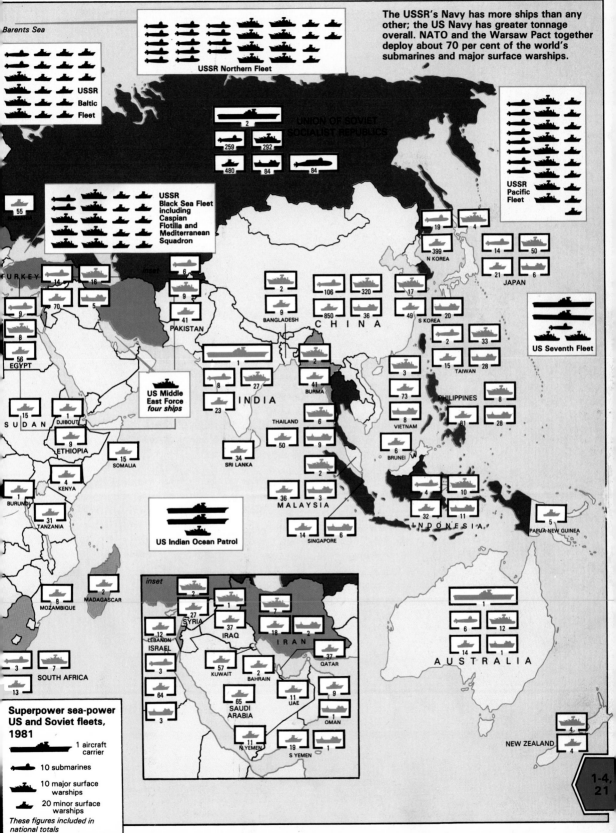

The USSR's Navy has more ships than any other; the US Navy has greater tonnage overall. NATO and the Warsaw Pact together deploy about 70 per cent of the world's submarines and major surface warships.

Barents Sea

USSR Northern Fleet

USSR Baltic Fleet

USSR Pacific Fleet

UNION OF SOVIET SOCIALIST REPUBLICS
2
259   292
480   84   84

USSR Black Sea Fleet including Caspian Flotilla and Mediterranean Squadron

55

US Seventh Fleet

N KOREA
19   4
399
14   50
21   6
JAPAN

TURKEY
14   16
9   70
5

inset
6
9
41
PAKISTAN

BANGLADESH
2
9
106   320
850   36
17
49   20
S KOREA

CHINA

EGYPT
9
8
56

SUDAN
15

DJIBOUTI   1
ETHIOPIA
SOMALIA   15
KENYA   4
BURUNDI   1
TANZANIA   31

US Middle East Force four ships

INDIA
1
8   27
23

BURMA
2
41

THAILAND
6
50   9

SRI LANKA
34

S KOREA
2   33
15   28
TAIWAN

PHILIPPINES
3
73
81   28
8

VIETNAM
6
8

BRUNEI
6

MALAYSIA
36
2

INDONESIA
4   10
32   11

PAPUA NEW GUINEA
5

US Indian Ocean Patrol

SINGAPORE
14   6

MOZAMBIQUE
8
MADAGASCAR   2

SOUTH AFRICA
3   7
13

inset
2
SYRIA   27
LEBANON   12
ISRAEL
IRAQ   37
1
7
18   2
IRAN   37
QATAR

KUWAIT   57
BAHRAIN   2
3
SAUDI ARABIA   64
65
3
UAE   11   9
OMAN   1
N YEMEN   11
S YEMEN   19   1

AUSTRALIA
1
6   12
14   1

NEW ZEALAND
4
4

Superpower sea-power US and Soviet fleets, 1981

1 aircraft carrier

10 submarines

10 major surface warships

20 minor surface warships

These figures included in national totals

1-4, 21

Part Three: Global Reach

The major rifts in world politics are defined by the international military order. At its core is the cold war – the superpowers' rivalry for global influence and the confrontation of their respective blocs. Economic and political ties bring other states into the orbit of one side or the other. The cold war is in continuous flux as each superpower modifies its policies, seeking to gain new advantage and bring more states within its sphere of influence. The few that have succeeded in remaining outside the superpowers' camps by exploiting the competition between them are constantly courted, sometimes threatened.

There is no doubting the West's predominance in world affairs. But alliances and allegiances are not carved in granite. External and internal pressures on numerous states threaten their alignment, or their non-alignment. Many states have changed allegiance; some have been veritable shuttlecocks between the two sides. The division of the world in 1982 is shown in *Map 16: Camps and Followers*.

Although Western influence is more widespread and in many ways far deeper than that of the USSR, it is less unified. The Western camp is riven by internal disputes and rivalries, all the more intense in the crisis and recession of the late 1970s and early 1980s. The core states of the Western military alliance are more sharply divided than at any time since 1945 over major political and economic issues. And within those countries, there are growing challenges to both the international military order and their national positions within it.

The components of the order are not locked in place simply by treaty and agreement. The foreign bases maintained by the major states, shown in *Map 17: A Corner of a Foreign Field* are more than the material manifestation of alliance, willing or enforced. They provide the possibility of far-flung military intervention in regional and national politics. For the states which host these bases, it is no light matter to ask their guests to leave before they are ready to go.

Alliance and division are also locked in place internally within armed forces, by the internationalisation of military education and training. In *Map 18: With a Little Help from their Friends*, we show what we have been able to unearth of the multiple linkages up, down and across the international hierarchy of armed force.

The first maps in this section reveal the extent of the West's global influence. Yet the USSR is not weak. *Map 19: The Soviet Garrison* depicts this strength, but the contrast with *Map 20: The US Network*, is telling. The USSR's major military strength is heavily concentrated, in the USSR itself and in contiguous states. The USA's military strength is more widespread. Its global presence is infinitely greater. Its watchful eyes and integrated international communication system surround the USSR. Based on a more thrusting economic system, the USA's reach is more effortless and the USSR's, therefore, all the more determined.

Presence itself provides power. Where that is not enough, military strength can be used for coercion, short of war, by shows of force (see *Map 21: Force Without War*). In war, the military as an instrument of policy show a crushing directness and crudity. But that is only part of the repertoire: in other situations, the military instrument can be used with finesse.

It is not easy for any state to escape the embrace of one or other side in the cold war. China is the most powerful of the non-aligned states. *Map 22: China: The Middle Kingdom* stresses its strategic role between the superpowers, and shows its massive armed forces and considerable military-industrial infrastructure. But the quantum leap to being a superpower comparable to the USA or USSR could be made, this century, only with assistance from abroad. The international military order restricts political options: states which would command power on the world stage must learn to play according to rules set by those which now dominate.

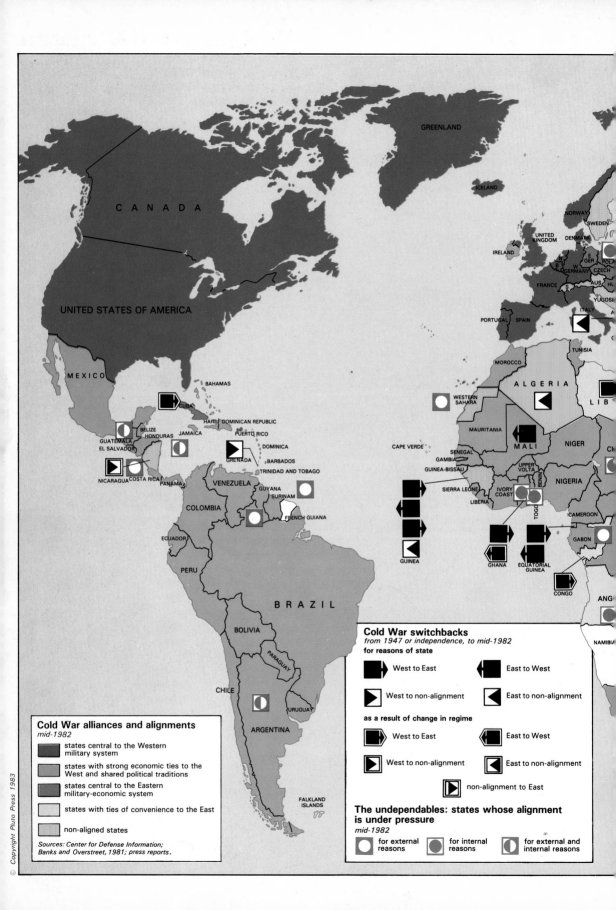

GREENLAND

ICELAND

NORWAY
SWEDEN

CANADA

UNITED
KINGDOM DENMARK

IRELAND

B
E GER
W POLA
GERMANY CZECH
S AUS HU
FRANCE YUGOSI

UNITED STATES OF AMERICA

PORTUGAL SPAIN ITALY

TUNISIA

MEXICO

BAHAMAS

MOROCCO

WESTERN
SAHARA

ALGERIA LIB

CUBA

HAITI DOMINICAN REPUBLIC

PUERTO RICO

MAURITANIA

MALI NIGER

BELIZE
HONDURAS JAMAICA
GUATEMALA
EL SALVADOR DOMINICA

CAPE VERDE

SENEGAL
GAMBIA
GUINEA-BISSAU

UPPER
VOLTA BENIN
NIGERIA

CH

GRENADA
BARBADOS
TRINIDAD AND TOBAGO

SIERRA LEONE
LIBERIA

IVORY
COAST

NICARAGUA COSTA RICA
PANAMA

VENEZUELA
GUYANA
SURINAM

TOGO

CAMEROON

COLOMBIA

FRENCH GUIANA

GUINEA

GHANA
EQUATORIAL
GUINEA

GABON

ECUADOR

CONGO

ANG

PERU

BRAZIL

NAMIBIA

BOLIVIA

Cold War switchbacks
from 1947 or independence, to mid-1982
for reasons of state

PARAGUAY

CHILE

West to East

East to West

URUGUAY

West to non-alignment

East to non-alignment

ARGENTINA

as a result of change in regime

West to East

East to West

Cold War alliances and alignments
mid-1982

West to non-alignment

East to non-alignment

states central to the Western
military system

non-alignment to East

states with strong economic ties to the
West and shared political traditions

FALKLAND
ISLANDS

states central to the Eastern
military-economic system

**The undependables: states whose alignment
is under pressure**
mid-1982

states with ties of convenience to the East

non-aligned states

for external
reasons

for internal
reasons

for external and
internal reasons

*Sources: Center for Defense Information;
Banks and Overstreet, 1981; press reports.*

Twenty-eight states have switched camps since the onset of the Cold War, some of them more than once. Many more are unreliable allies.

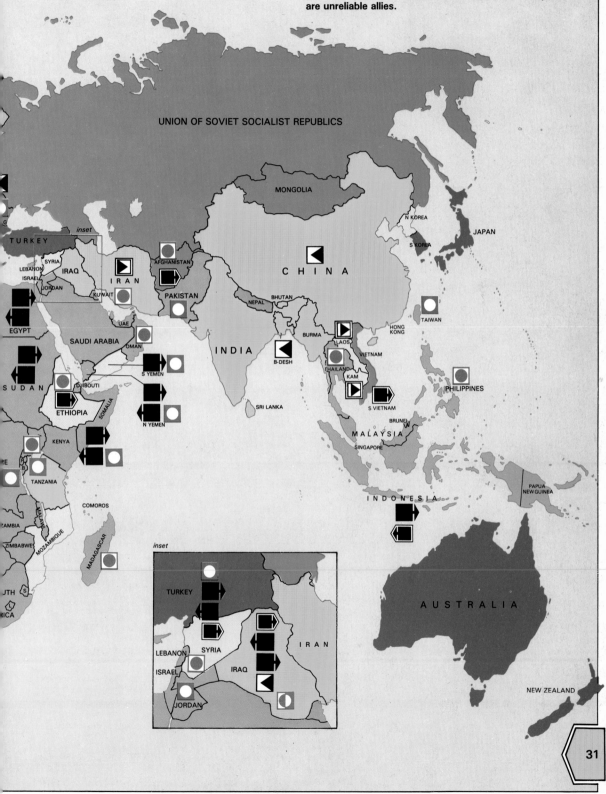

UNION OF SOVIET SOCIALIST REPUBLICS

MONGOLIA

N KOREA

JAPAN

S KOREA

inset

TURKEY

SYRIA

LEBANON

IRAQ

ISRAEL

JORDAN

EGYPT

KUWAIT

IRAN

AFGHANISTAN

PAKISTAN

NEPAL

BHUTAN

CHINA

TAIWAN

HONG KONG

UAE

SAUDI ARABIA

OMAN

INDIA

BURMA

LAOS

VIETNAM

S YEMEN

B-DESH

THAILAND

KAM

PHILIPPINES

SUDAN

DJIBOUTI

ETHIOPIA

SOMALIA

N YEMEN

SRI LANKA

S VIETNAM

BRUNEI

KENYA

MALAYSIA

SINGAPORE

INDONESIA

PAPUA NEW GUINEA

TANZANIA

COMOROS

MADAGASCAR

MALAWI

AMBIA

ZIMBABWE

MOZAMBIQUE

AUSTRALIA

JTH

RICA

inset

TURKEY

LEBANON

SYRIA

IRAN

ISRAEL

IRAQ

JORDAN

NEW ZEALAND

31

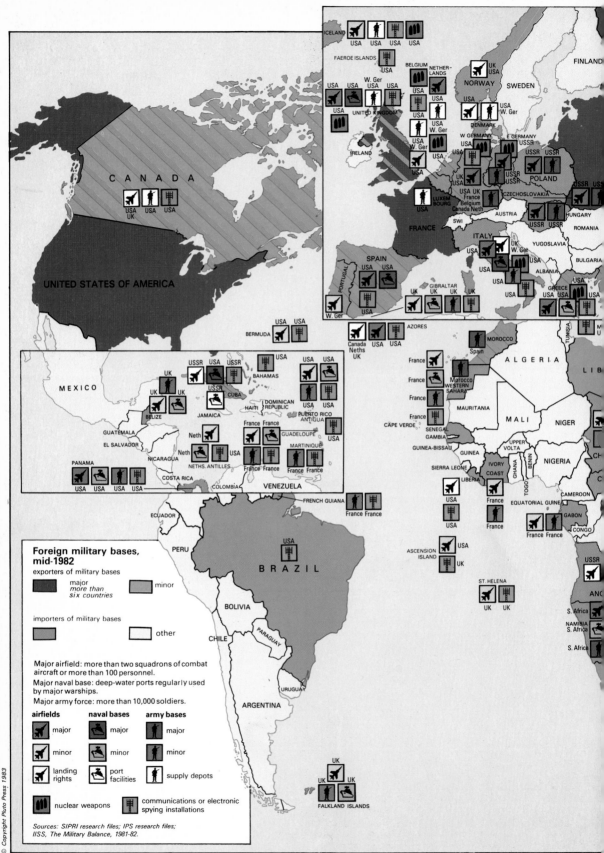

Foreign military bases, mid-1982

exporters of military bases

major
*more than
six countries*

minor

importers of military bases

other

Major airfield: more than two squadrons of combat aircraft or more than 100 personnel.
Major naval base: deep-water ports regularly used by major warships.
Major army force: more than 10,000 soldiers.

airfields	naval bases	army bases
major	major	major
minor	minor	minor
landing rights	port facilities	supply depots

nuclear weapons

communications or electronic spying installations

Sources: SIPRI research files; IPS research files;
IISS, The Military Balance, 1981-82.

There are about 3000 foreign military
bases and installations world-wide.

UNION OF SOVIET SOCIALIST REPUBLICS

SVALBARD

SR

USSR USSR
MONGOLIA

SOUTHERN
KURILES
USSR USSR USSR

N KOREA

JAPAN
USA USA USA USA

S KOREA
USA

USA

IWO JIMA
USA USA

CYPRUS

SYRIA
inset

EGYPT

IRAQ

KUWAIT

IRAN

PAKISTAN

USSR USSR
AFGHANISTAN

CHINA

BHUTAN
India

NEPAL

B-
DESH

MACAU
Portugal

HONG
KONG

LAOS

TAIWAN

Taiwan
UK UK UK UK

SAUDI ARABIA

BAHRAIN

UAE
OMAN
USA

USA
UK

INDIA

BURMA

Vietnam

VIETNAM

Philippines

Taiwan
Vietnam
Philippines

PHILIPPINES

USSR
N
YEMEN

S YEMEN

USSR USSR
France France France France

SUDAN
S. Yemen

DJIBOUTI

Cuba
ETHIOPIA

SOMALIA
USA USA

USA

USA
UK

THAILAND

KAM

Vietnam

SRI LANKA

USSR

BRUNEI

MALAYSIA

USA USA USA USA

UGANDA

KENYA

DIEGO GARCIA (UK)

France France France
COMOROS

Australia
New Zealand

Malaysia

New
Zealand

SINGAPORE

INDONESIA

PAPUA NEW GUINEA

TANZANIA

MALAWI

ZAMBIA

ZIMBABWE

MOZAMBIQUE

France
MADAGASCAR

France

SOUTH
AFRICA

MONGOLIA

CHINA

JAPAN

Indonesia

EAST TIMOR

CHRISTMAS ISLAND
Australia

MARCUS
ISLANDS
USA

AUSTRALIA

UK
USA USA

GUAM
USA USA USA

USA
MICRONESIA

INDONESIA

USA USA
MIDWAY
ISLAND

USA USA
JOHNSTON ATOLL

USA USA
MARSHALL ISLANDS

AUSTRALIA

NEW
CALEDONIA
France France

France France

USA USA
AMERICAN
SAMOA

France France
FRENCH POLYNESIA

NEW ZEALAND
USA USA USA

inset

CYPRUS

LEB

Syria
Israel

UK
Greece
Turkey

UK
Greece
Turkey

UK

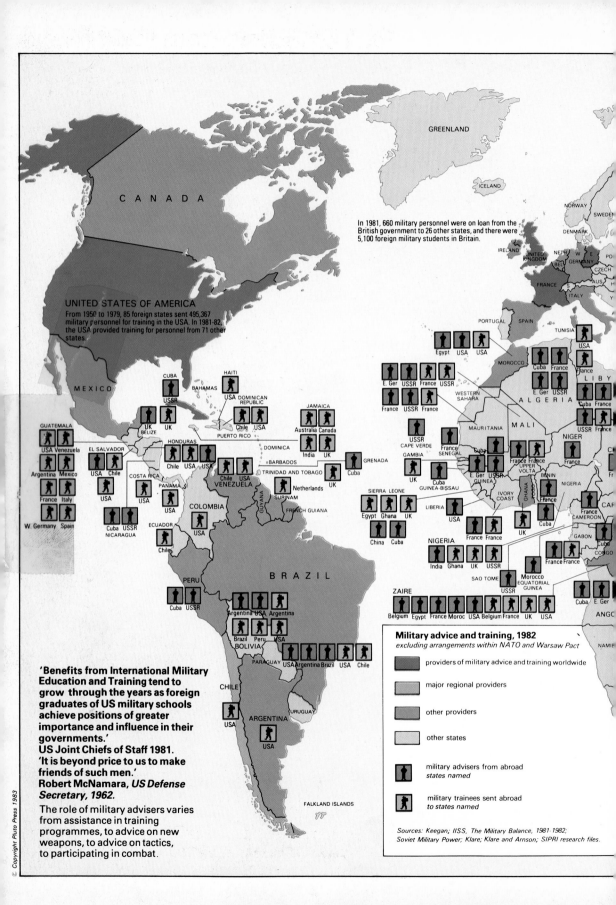

GREENLAND

ICELAND

NORWAY SWEDE

DENMARK

IRELAND NETH PO
UNITED W E
KINGDOM GERMANY CZECH
BEL
FRANCE S AUS
ITALY Y

In 1981, 660 military personnel were on loan from the
British government to 26 other states, and there were
5,100 foreign military students in Britain.

CANADA

UNITED STATES OF AMERICA
From 1950 to 1979, 85 foreign states sent 495,367
military personnel for training in the USA. In 1981-82,
the USA provided training for personnel from 71 other
states.

PORTUGAL SPAIN

TUNISIA

Egypt USA USA

MOROCCO

Cuba France

MEXICO

CUBA HAITI
USSR BAHAMAS USA DOMINICAN
REPUBLIC

JAMAICA

Australia Canada

India UK

E. Ger USSR France USSR

France USSR France

WESTERN
SAHARA

E. Ger USSR

France France LIBYA

ALGERIA

Cuba France

USSR France

UK USA
BELIZE

Chile USA
PUERTO RICO

DOMINICA

USSR
CAPE VERDE

MAURITANIA

MALI

France
Cuba

NIGER

France

GUATEMALA

USA Venezuela

EL SALVADOR

USA Chile

HONDURAS

Chile USA USA

Chile USA

VENEZUELA

GRENADA

Cuba

France
SENEGAL France France UPPER BENIN
GAMBIA VOLTA
E. Ger USSR NIGERIA

Argentina Mexico

France Italy

COSTA RICA

USA

PANAMA

USA

BARBADOS
TRINIDAD AND TOBAGO

Netherlands

SURINAM

Cuba
GUINEA-BISSAU

UK
SIERRA LEONE

IVORY
COAST
GHANA
France
UK

France

NIGERIA

France France

W. Germany Spain

COLOMBIA

FRENCH GUIANA

Egypt Ghana UK

Cuba
LIBERIA

USA

Cuba
CAMEROON
France

GABON

Cuba

Cuba USSR

ECUADOR

NICARAGUA

USA

China Cuba

NIGERIA

France France
CONGO

Chile

India Ghana UK USSR

SAO TOME
EQUATORIAL
GUINEA

Morocco
USSR

Cuba E. Ger

PERU

BRAZIL

ZAIRE

NAMIB

Cuba USSR

Argentina USA Argentina

Brazil Peru USA

BOLIVIA

Belgium Egypt France Moroc USA Belgium France UK USA

ANGO

PARAGUAY

USA Argentina Brazil USA Chile

Military advice and training, 1982
excluding arrangements within NATO and Warsaw Pact

providers of military advice and training worldwide

major regional providers

other providers

other states

military advisers from abroad
states named

military trainees sent abroad
to states named

CHILE

USA

URUGUAY

ARGENTINA

USA

'Benefits from International Military
Education and Training tend to
grow through the years as foreign
graduates of US military schools
achieve positions of greater
importance and influence in their
governments.'
US Joint Chiefs of Staff 1981.
'It is beyond price to us to make
friends of such men.'
Robert McNamara, *US Defense
Secretary, 1962.*

The role of military advisers varies
from assistance in training
programmes, to advice on new
weapons, to advice on tactics,
to participating in combat.

FALKLAND ISLANDS

Sources: Keegan; IISS, The Military Balance, 1981-1982;
Soviet Military Power; Klare; Klare and Arnson; SIPRI research files.

© Copyright Pluto Press 1983

Twenty-one states send military advisers to other countries. Thirty-one states take military trainees from other countries.

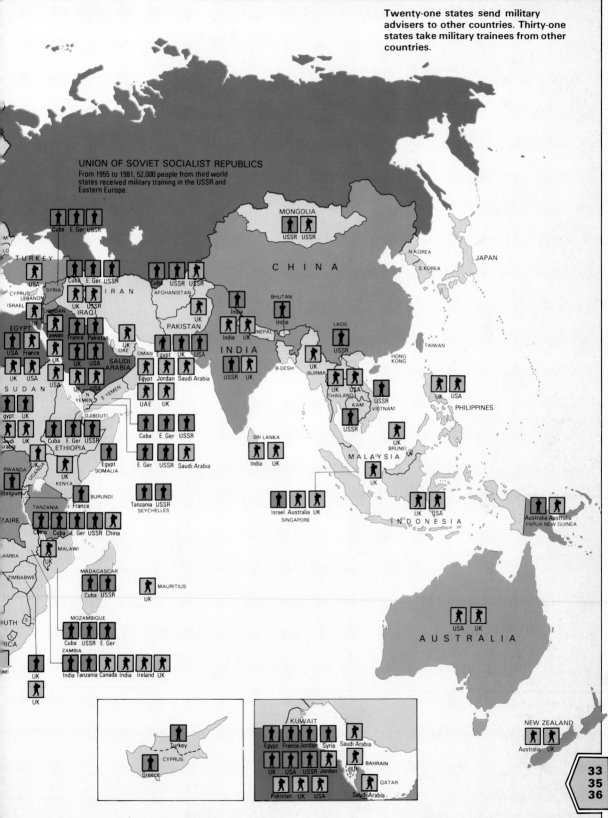

UNION OF SOVIET SOCIALIST REPUBLICS
From 1955 to 1981, 52,000 people from third world states received military training in the USSR and Eastern Europe.

Cuba E.Ger USSR

MONGOLIA
USSR USSR

CHINA

N.KOREA
S.KOREA

JAPAN

TURKEY
USA
CYPRUS
LEBANON
ISRAEL
SYRIA
JORDAN
Cuba E.Ger USSR
UK USSR
IRAQ
IRAN
AFGHANISTAN
Cuba USSR USSR
PAKISTAN
UK
UK
UAE

BHUTAN
India
India
India UK
NEPAL

LAOS
USSR

TAIWAN

HONG KONG

EGYPT
USA France
UK
UK USA
USA
SAUDI ARABIA
Egypt UK USA
OMAN
Egypt Jordan Saudi Arabia
INDIA
USSR UK
B-DESH
UK BURMA
UK USA
THAILAND
USSR VIETNAM

SUDAN
gypt UK
N YEMEN
UAE UK
S.YEMEN
Cuba E.Ger USSR
KAM
USSR
UK
BRUNEI
PHILIPPINES

Saudi Araba
Egypt UK
RWANDA
UGANDA
UK
KENYA
ETHIOPIA
Egypt SOMALIA
E.Ger USSR Saudi Arabia

SRI LANKA
India UK

MALAYSIA
UK
UK USA
INDONESIA

Belgium
BURUNDI
TANZANIA France
Tanzania USSR
SEYCHELLES

Israel Australia UK
SINGAPORE

Australia Australia
PAPUA NEW GUINEA

ZAIRE
China Cuba E.Ger USSR China
AMBIA
MALAWI
UK
ZIMBABWE
MADAGASCAR
Cuba USSR
MAURITIUS
UK

AUSTRALIA

UTH
S
RICA
el UK
MOZAMBIQUE
Cuba USSR E.Ger
ZAMBIA
India Tanzania Canada India Ireland UK
UK

USA UK

UK

NEW ZEALAND
Australia UK

Turkey
CYPRUS
Greece

KUWAIT
Egypt France Jordan Syria Saudi Arabia
UK USA USSR Jordan
BAHRAIN
Pakistan UK USA
QATAR
Saudi Arabia

33
35
36

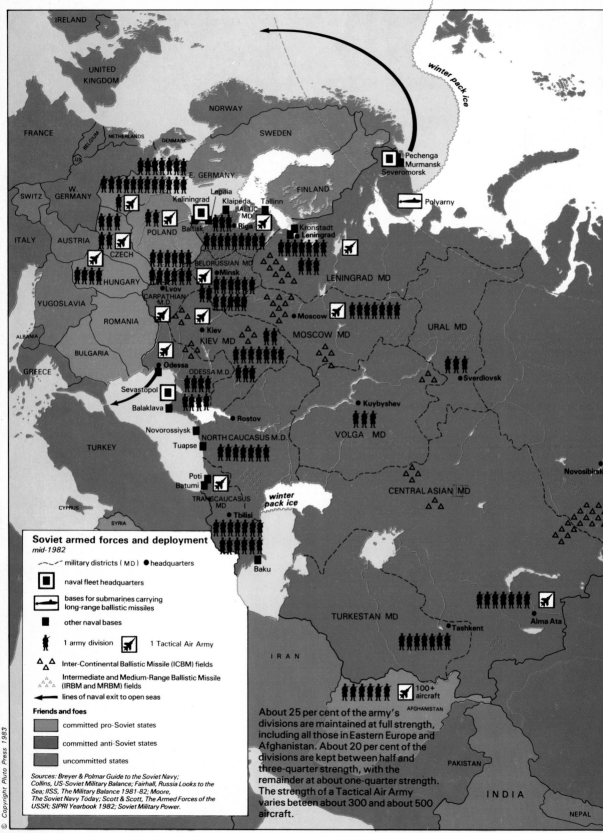

Soviet armed forces and deployment
mid-1982

- ⌐⌐⌐ ● military districts (M D) ● headquarters
- ▣ naval fleet headquarters
- ⊏⊐ bases for submarines carrying long-range ballistic missiles
- ■ other naval bases
- 👤 1 army division   ✈ 1 Tactical Air Army
- △△△ Inter-Continental Ballistic Missile (ICBM) fields
- △△△ Intermediate and Medium-Range Ballistic Missile (IRBM and MRBM) fields
- ← lines of naval exit to open seas

Friends and foes

- committed pro-Soviet states
- committed anti-Soviet states
- uncommitted states

Sources: Breyer & Polmar Guide to the Soviet Navy; Collins, US-Soviet Military Balance; Fairhall, Russia Looks to the Sea; IISS, The Military Balance 1981-82; Moore, The Soviet Navy Today; Scott & Scott, The Armed Forces of the USSR; SIPRI Yearbook 1982; Soviet Military Power.

About 25 per cent of the army's divisions are maintained at full strength, including all those in Eastern Europe and Afghanistan. About 20 per cent of the divisions are kept between half and three-quarter strength, with the remainder at about one-quarter strength. The strength of a Tactical Air Army varies beteen about 300 and about 500 aircraft.

✈ 100+ aircraft

© Copyright Pluto Press 1983

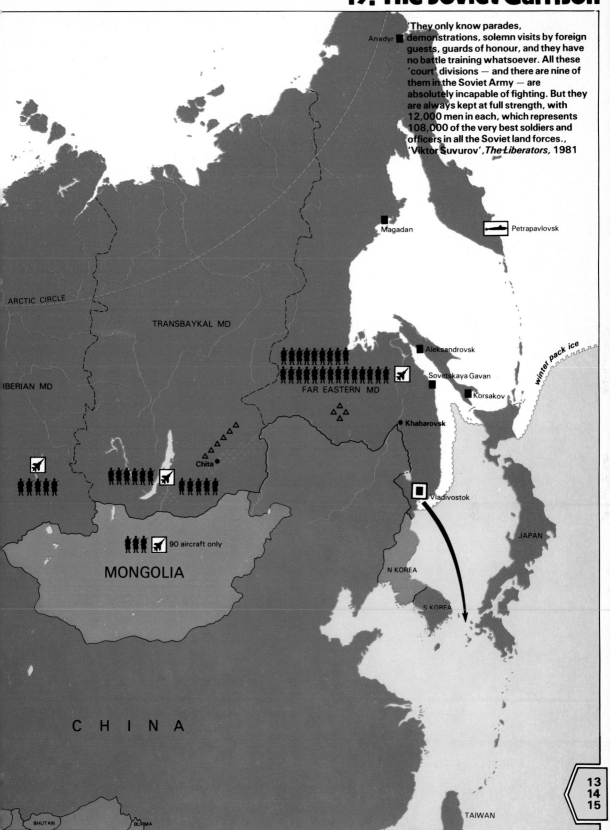

'They only know parades, demonstrations, solemn visits by foreign guests, guards of honour, and they have no battle training whatsoever. All these 'court' divisions — and there are nine of them in the Soviet Army — are absolutely incapable of fighting. But they are always kept at full strength, with 12,000 men in each, which represents 108,000 of the very best soldiers and officers in all the Soviet land forces., 'Viktor Suvurov', *The Liberators*, 1981

Anadyr

ARCTIC CIRCLE

TRANSBAYKAL MD

Magadan

Petrapavlovsk

Aleksandrovsk

Sovetskaya Gavan

winter pack ice

IBERIAN MD

FAR EASTERN MD

Korsakov

Khabarovsk

Chita

Vladivostok

JAPAN

N KOREA

90 aircraft only

MONGOLIA

S KOREA

C H I N A

BHUTAN   BURMA

TAIWAN

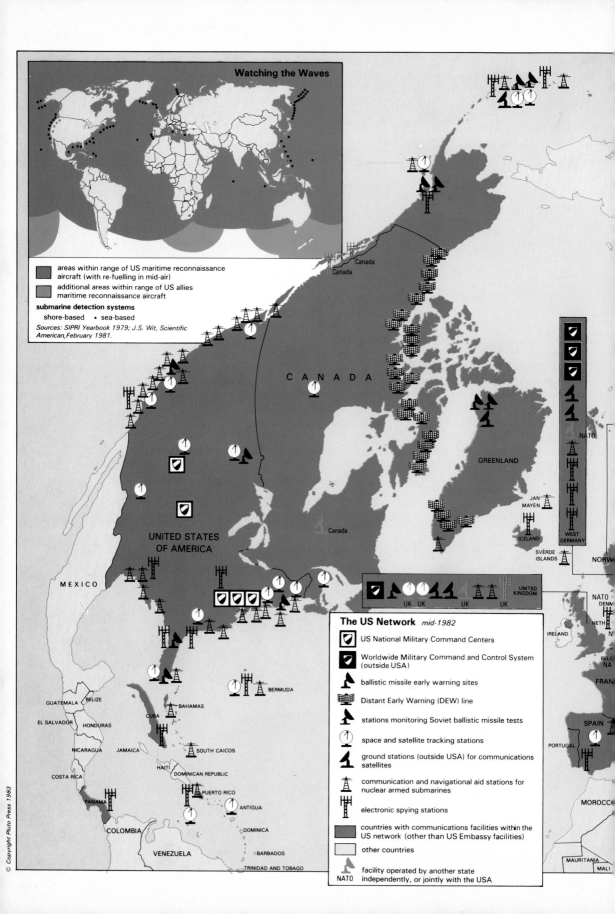

Watching the Waves

■ areas within range of US maritime reconnaissance
aircraft (with re-fuelling in mid-air)

▨ additional areas within range of US allies
maritime reconnaissance aircraft

submarine detection systems

— shore-based • sea-based

*Sources: SIPRI Yearbook 1979; J.S. Wit, Scientific
American, February 1981.*

C A N A D A

GREENLAND

JAN
MAYEN

ICELAND

SVERDE
ISLANDS

UNITED STATES
OF AMERICA

NATO

WEST
GERMANY

NORW

NATO
DENM

NETH

UNITED
KINGDOM

UK   UK   UK   UK

IRELAND

BELG
NA

FRAN

MEXICO

GUATEMALA   BELIZE

EL SALVADOR   HONDURAS

NICARAGUA   JAMAICA

COSTA RICA

PANAMA

COLOMBIA

CUBA   BAHAMAS

HAITI

DOMINICAN REPUBLIC

PUERTO RICO

ANTIGUA

DOMINICA

BARBADOS

TRINIDAD AND TOBAGO

VENEZUELA

SOUTH CAICOS

BERMUDA

SPAIN

PORTUGAL

MOROCCO

MAURITANIA   MALI

The US Network *mid-1982*

US National Military Command Centers

Worldwide Military Command and Control System
(outside USA)

ballistic missile early warning sites

Distant Early Warning (DEW) line

stations monitoring Soviet ballistic missile tests

space and satellite tracking stations

ground stations (outside USA) for communications
satellites

communication and navigational aid stations for
nuclear armed submarines

electronic spying stations

countries with communications facilities within the
US network (other than US Embassy facilities)

other countries

NATO   facility operated by another state
independently, or jointly with the USA

The USA's international system for information-gathering and communications is unrivalled. Satellite technology is beginning to free the system from the need for ground-based installations.

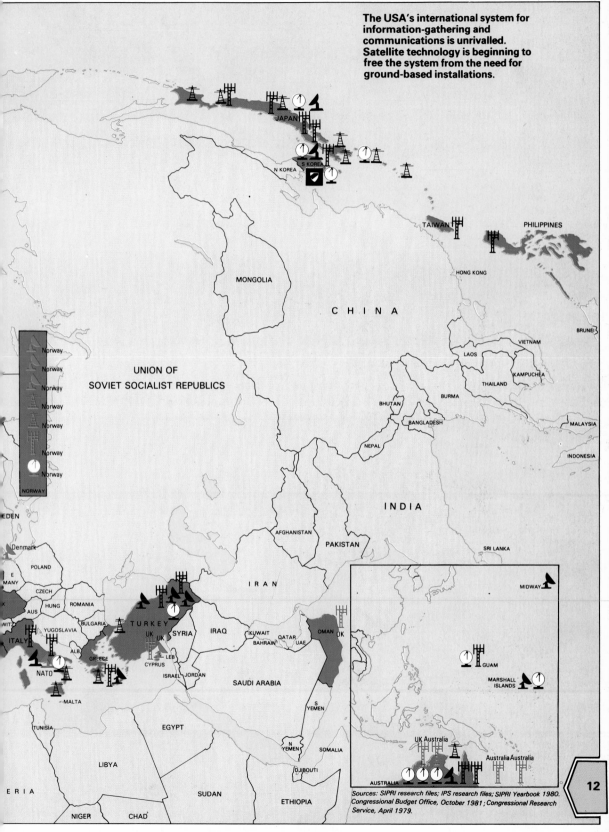

Sources: SIPRI research files; IPS research files; SIPRI Yearbook 1980. Congressional Budget Office, October 1981; Congressional Research Service, April 1979.

12

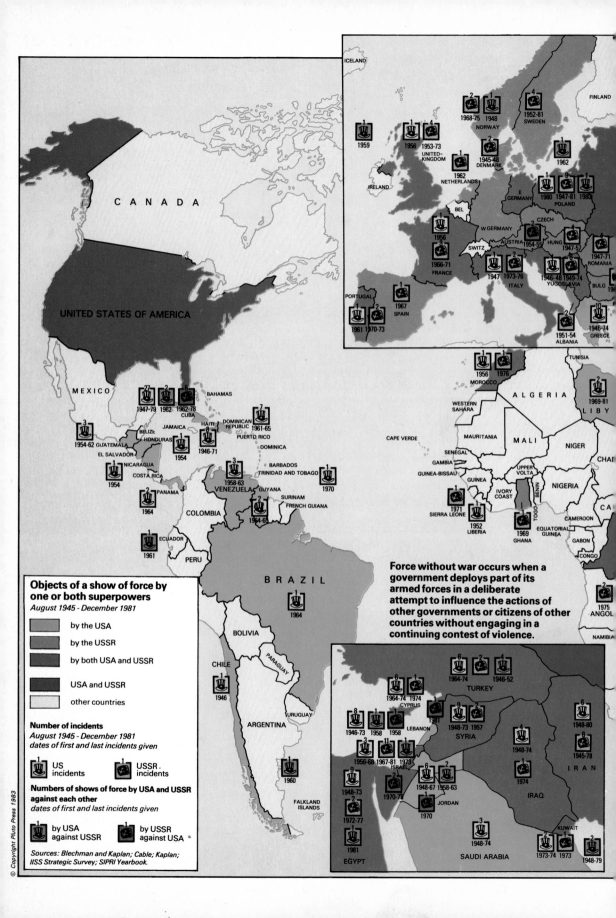

Force without war occurs when a government deploys part of its armed forces in a deliberate attempt to influence the actions of other governments or citizens of other countries without engaging in a continuing contest of violence.

Objects of a show of force by one or both superpowers

August 1945 - December 1981

- by the USA
- by the USSR
- by both USA and USSR
- USA and USSR
- other countries

Number of incidents

August 1945 - December 1981
dates of first and last incidents given

- US incidents
- USSR incidents

Numbers of shows of force by USA and USSR against each other

dates of first and last incidents given

- by USA against USSR
- by USSR against USA

Sources: Blechman and Kaplan; Cable; Kaplan; IISS Strategic Survey; SIPRI Yearbook.

© Copyright Pluto Press 1983

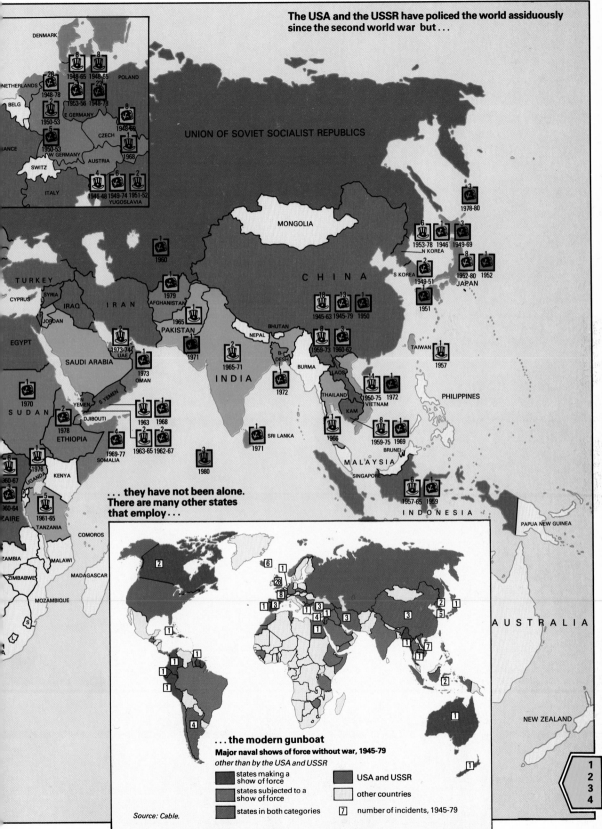

The USA and the USSR have policed the world assiduously since the second world war but . . .

. . . they have not been alone. There are many other states that employ . . .

. . . the modern gunboat
Major naval shows of force without war, 1945-79
other than by the USA and USSR

- states making a show of force
- states subjected to a show of force
- states in both categories
- USA and USSR
- other countries
- 7 number of incidents, 1945-79

Source: Cable.

1
2
3
4

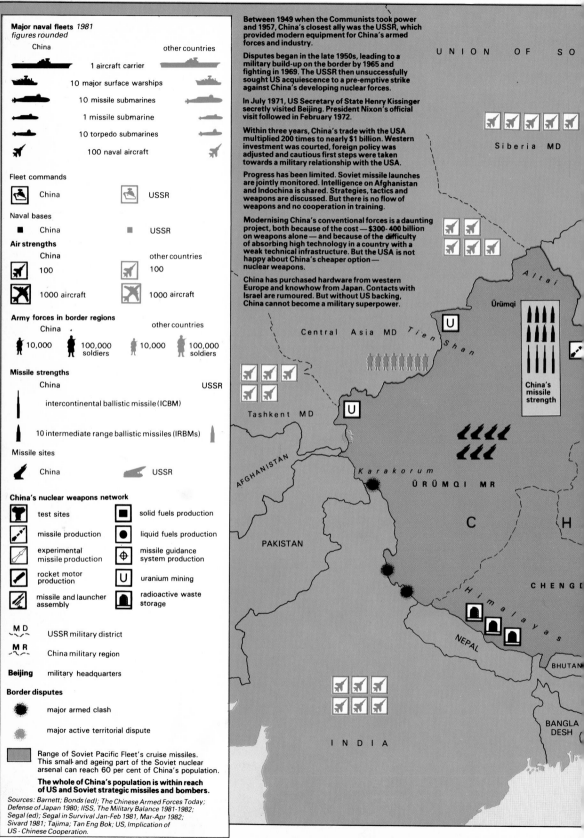

Major naval fleets *1981*
figures rounded

China		other countries
	1 aircraft carrier	
	10 major surface warships	
	10 missile submarines	
	1 missile submarine	
	10 torpedo submarines	
	100 naval aircraft	

Fleet commands

China   USSR

Naval bases

■ China   ■ USSR

Air strengths

China		other countries
	100	100
	1000 aircraft	1000 aircraft

Army forces in border regions

China		other countries	
10,000	100,000 soldiers	10,000	100,000 soldiers

Missile strengths

China   USSR

│ intercontinental ballistic missile (ICBM)

▌ 10 intermediate range ballistic missiles (IRBMs)

Missile sites

China   USSR

China's nuclear weapons network

	test sites	■	solid fuels production
	missile production	●	liquid fuels production
	experimental missile production	⊕	missile guidance system production
	rocket motor production	U	uranium mining
	missile and launcher assembly		radioactive waste storage

M D   USSR military district

M R   China military region

Beijing   military headquarters

Border disputes

● major armed clash

● major active territorial dispute

Range of Soviet Pacific Fleet's cruise missiles. This small and ageing part of the Soviet nuclear arsenal can reach 60 per cent of China's population.

The whole of China's population is within reach of US and Soviet strategic missiles and bombers.

Sources: Barnett; Bonds (ed); The Chinese Armed Forces Today; Defense of Japan 1980; IISS, The Military Balance 1981-1982; Segal (ed); Segal in Survival Jan-Feb 1981, Mar-Apr 1982; Sivard 1981; Tajima; Tan Eng Bok; US, Implication of US - Chinese Cooperation.

Between 1949 when the Communists took power and 1957, China's closest ally was the USSR, which provided modern equipment for China's armed forces and industry.

Disputes began in the late 1950s, leading to a military build-up on the border by 1965 and fighting in 1969. The USSR then unsuccessfully sought US acquiescence to a pre-emptive strike against China's developing nuclear forces.

In July 1971, US Secretary of State Henry Kissinger secretly visited Beijing. President Nixon's official visit followed in February 1972.

Within three years, China's trade with the USA multiplied 200 times to nearly $1 billion. Western investment was courted, foreign policy was adjusted and cautious first steps were taken towards a military relationship with the USA.

Progress has been limited. Soviet missile launches are jointly monitored. Intelligence on Afghanistan and Indochina is shared. Strategies, tactics and weapons are discussed. But there is no flow of weapons and no cooperation in training.

Modernising China's conventional forces is a daunting project, both because of the cost — $300- 400 billion on weapons alone — and because of the difficulty of absorbing high technology in a country with a weak technical infrastructure. But the USA is not happy about China's cheaper option — nuclear weapons.

China has purchased hardware from western Europe and knowhow from Japan. Contacts with Israel are rumoured. But without US backing, China cannot become a military superpower.

UNION   OF   SO

Siberia MD

Altai

Ürümqi

U

Central Asia MD   Tien Shan

China's missile strength

Tashkent MD

U

AFGHANISTAN   Karakorum   ÜRÜMQI MR

C   H

PAKISTAN

CHENGD

Himalayas

NEPAL

BHUTAN

INDIA   BANGLA DESH

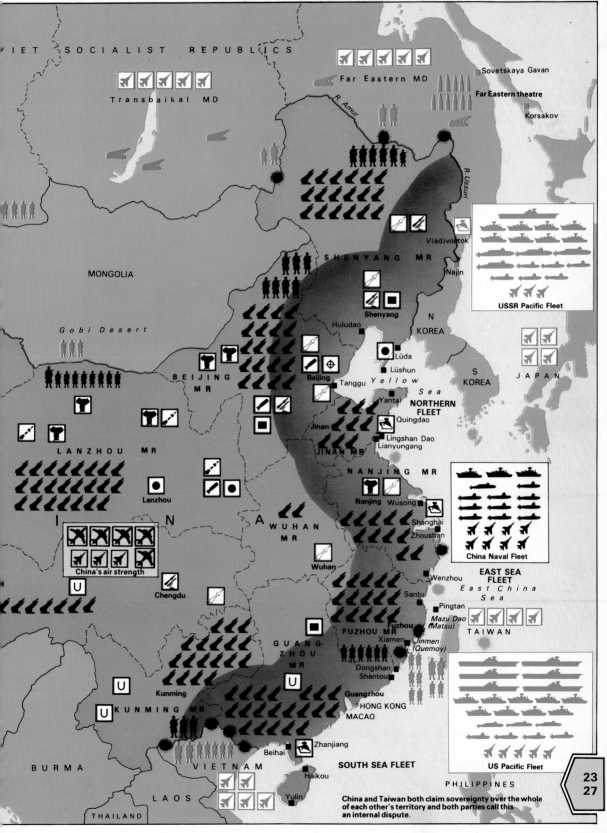

VIET SOCIALIST REPUBLICS

Transbaikal MD

Far Eastern MD

Sovetskaya Gavan

Far Eastern theatre

Korsakov

R. Amur

R. Ussuri

Vladivostok

Najin

SHENYANG MR

MONGOLIA

Gobi Desert

Shenyang

Huludao

N KOREA

USSR Pacific Fleet

Lüda

Lüshun

Tanggu

Yellow

Sea

S KOREA

JAPAN

BEIJING MR

Beijing

Yantai

NORTHERN FLEET

Quingdao

Jinan

Lingshan Dao

Lianyungang

LANZHOU MR

Lanzhou

JINAN MR

NANJING MR

Nanjing

Wusong

Shanghai

Zhoushan

I N A

WUHAN MR

China Naval Fleet

China's air strength

Wuhan

EAST SEA FLEET

East China Sea

U

Chengdu

Wenzhou

Santu

Pingtan

Mazu Dao (Matsu)

TAIWAN

FUZHOU MR

Fuzhou

Xiamen

Jinmen (Quemoy)

GUANG ZHOU MR

U

Dongshan

Shantou

Kunming

Guangzhou

U

KUNMING MR

HONG KONG

MACAO

U

Zhanjiang

Beihai

SOUTH SEA FLEET

BURMA

VIETNAM

Haikou

US Pacific Fleet

LAOS

Yulin

PHILIPPINES

China and Taiwan both claim sovereignty over the whole of each other's territory and both parties call this an internal dispute.

THAILAND

23
27

Part Four: Resources

Armed conflicts and armed peace are not cheap. The military have a great appetite for resources of every kind, from base metals to the highest flights of scientific imagination. They command a storehouse of skills and knowledge among the approximately 80 million people who work in and for the armed forces.

The quantity and sophistication of resources devoted to the international military order are thrown into sharper relief when contrasted with what is available for other uses. To take a modest example, a single air-to-air missile can cost as much as the annual livelihood of 10,000 inhabitants of a country such as

Bhutan. Rich states spend on official development aid to poor states less than half of one per cent of annual military spending worldwide. The contrast between the wealth devoted to military purposes and the poverty of much of humanity is obvious and notorious. It is a standing indictment of utterly distorted priorities.

The economic effects of military spending remain a matter of controversy. There is an argument that the concentration of high technology in the military sector produces beneficial 'spin-offs' for civil industry. Examples over the years range from assembly-line production, through nuclear power, to computers and integrated circuits. Yet this suggests that had the same energies been devoted to civil technology, the same results could have been gained. What is undeniable is that resources used for one purpose are unavailable for others. And certainly, among western states, those which have spent the highest proportions of their national wealth on arms have recorded the lowest economic growth rates.

The proportion of the world total spent on arms by each state is shown in *Map 23: Hey, Big Spender*. The cartogram technique used for this map reveals the hierarchy of the international military order. But the highest rates of increase in military spending tend to be found among the less elevated members of the hierarchy. The bigger proportions of national wealth devoted to arms spending tend to be found among the same states (see *Map 24: The Military Bite*). These states effectively seek a reordering of the global or regional hierarchy of military power. But in doing so, they follow the technological fashions set by the superpowers and their strongest allies. They thus aid the more powerful by providing a market for sophisticated weapons, and the gap between the superpowers and the rest remains enormous (see *Map 25: Goliaths*). Increased arms spending by some of the lesser states serves only to entrench the international military order. It makes nobody safer, and makes most of us poorer.

Even the superpowers' military machines can no longer be supplied entirely from their own or allied sources. They draw upon each other for some essentials. Part of this process is revealed in *Map 28: Shuttle Service*. And this serves to underline a crucial element of the international military order. There is an underlying unity between its major actors, even as they confront each other with the threat of ultimate destruction. The insecurity that each creates for the other creates in turn further insecurity which each requires to justify its existence. They feed upon each other. They collude in competition, collaborate in confrontation. They are the worst of enemies, and yet they need each other.

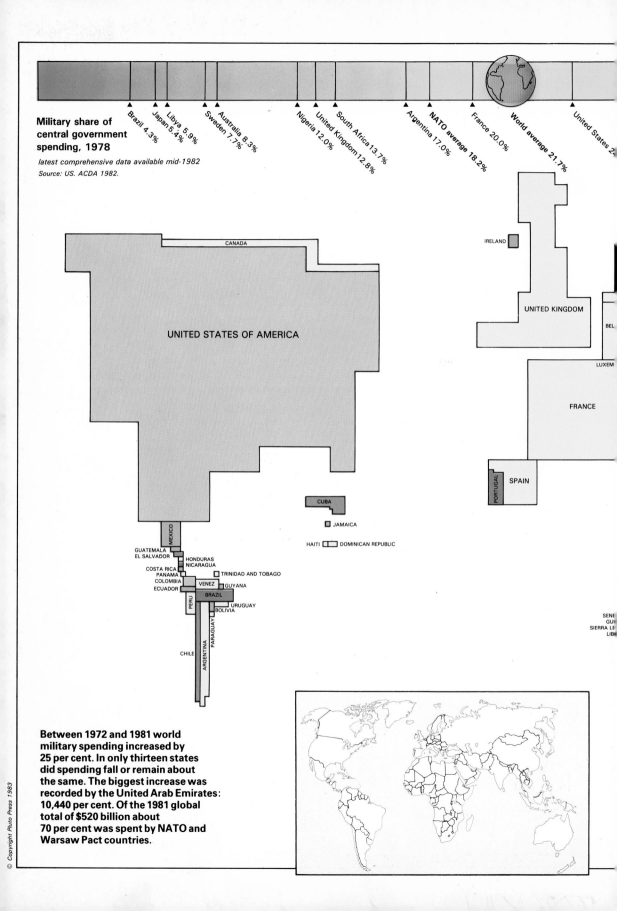

Military share of central government spending, 1978

latest comprehensive data available mid-1982
Source: US. ACDA 1982.

Brazil 4.3%
Japan 5.4%
Libya 5.9%
Sweden 7.7%
Australia 8.3%
Nigeria 12.0%
United Kingdom 12.8%
South Africa 13.7%
Argentina 17.0%
NATO average 18.2%
France 20.0%
World average 21.7%
United States 2

CANADA

UNITED STATES OF AMERICA

CUBA

JAMAICA

HAITI DOMINICAN REPUBLIC

MEXICO

GUATEMALA
EL SALVADOR
HONDURAS
NICARAGUA
COSTA RICA
PANAMA
COLOMBIA
ECUADOR
VENEZ
GUYANA
TRINIDAD AND TOBAGO
PERU
BRAZIL
URUGUAY
BOLIVIA
ARGENTINA
PARAGUAY
CHILE

IRELAND

UNITED KINGDOM

BEL

LUXEM

FRANCE

PORTUGAL SPAIN

SENE
GUI
SIERRA LE
LIB

Between 1972 and 1981 world military spending increased by 25 per cent. In only thirteen states did spending fall or remain about the same. The biggest increase was recorded by the United Arab Emirates: 10,440 per cent. Of the 1981 global total of $520 billion about 70 per cent was spent by NATO and Warsaw Pact countries.

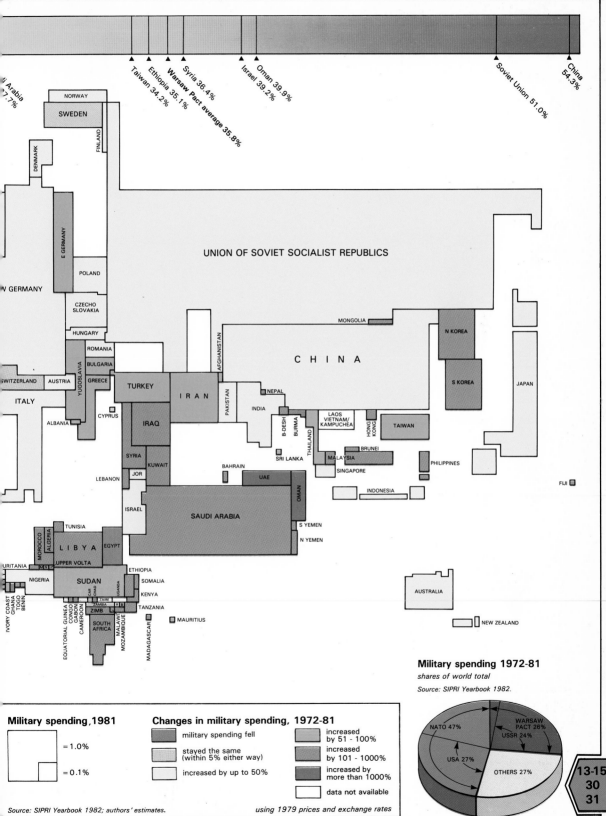

Taiwan 34.2%
Ethiopia 35.1%
Warsaw Pact average 35.8%
Syria 36.4%
Israel 39.2%
Oman 39.9%
Soviet Union 51.0%
China 54.3%

NORWAY
SWEDEN
FINLAND
DENMARK
E GERMANY
W GERMANY
POLAND
CZECHO SLOVAKIA
HUNGARY
ROMANIA
YUGOSLAVIA
BULGARIA
SWITZERLAND
AUSTRIA
GREECE
ITALY
ALBANIA

UNION OF SOVIET SOCIALIST REPUBLICS

MONGOLIA
N KOREA
S KOREA
JAPAN
CHINA
AFGHANISTAN
TURKEY
IRAN
PAKISTAN
NEPAL
INDIA
CYPRUS
IRAQ
SYRIA
KUWAIT
B-DESH
BURMA
THAILAND
LAOS VIETNAM/ KAMPUCHEA
HONG KONG
TAIWAN
SRI LANKA
MALAYSIA
BRUNEI
SINGAPORE
PHILIPPINES
LEBANON
JOR
BAHRAIN
UAE
OMAN
INDONESIA
FIJI
ISRAEL
SAUDI ARABIA
S YEMEN
N YEMEN
TUNISIA
MOROCCO
ALGERIA
LIBYA
EGYPT
URITANIA
UPPER VOLTA
NIGERIA
SUDAN
ETHIOPIA
SOMALIA
KENYA
IVORY COAST
GHANA
TOGO
BENIN
EQUATORIAL GUINEA
CONGO
GABON
CAMEROON
CAR
CHAD
ZAIRE
UGANDA
ZAMBIA
ZIMB
TANZANIA
MALAWI
MOZAMBIQUE
MADAGASCAR
MAURITIUS
SOUTH AFRICA
AUSTRALIA
NEW ZEALAND

Military spending 1972-81
shares of world total
Source: SIPRI Yearbook 1982.

NATO 47%
WARSAW PACT 26%
USSR 24%
USA 27%
OTHERS 27%

Military spending, 1981

= 1.0%
= 0.1%

Changes in military spending, 1972-81

military spending fell
stayed the same (within 5% either way)
increased by up to 50%
increased by 51 - 100%
increased by 101 - 1000%
increased by more than 1000%
data not available

Source: SIPRI Yearbook 1982; authors' estimates.

using 1979 prices and exchange rates

13-15
30
31

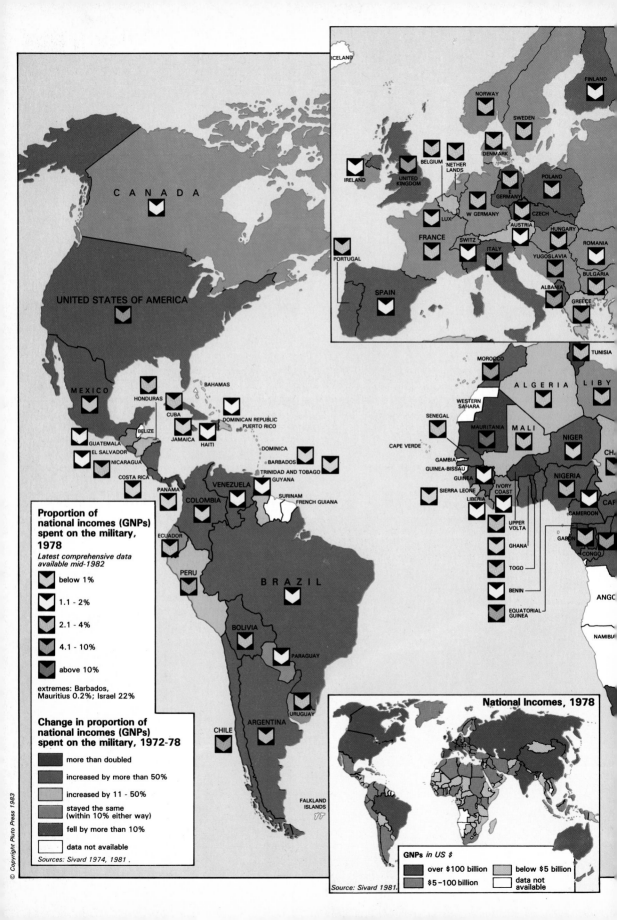

'The cost of a ten year programme to provide for essential food and health needs in developing countries is less than half of one year's military spending.' The Brandt Report, 1980

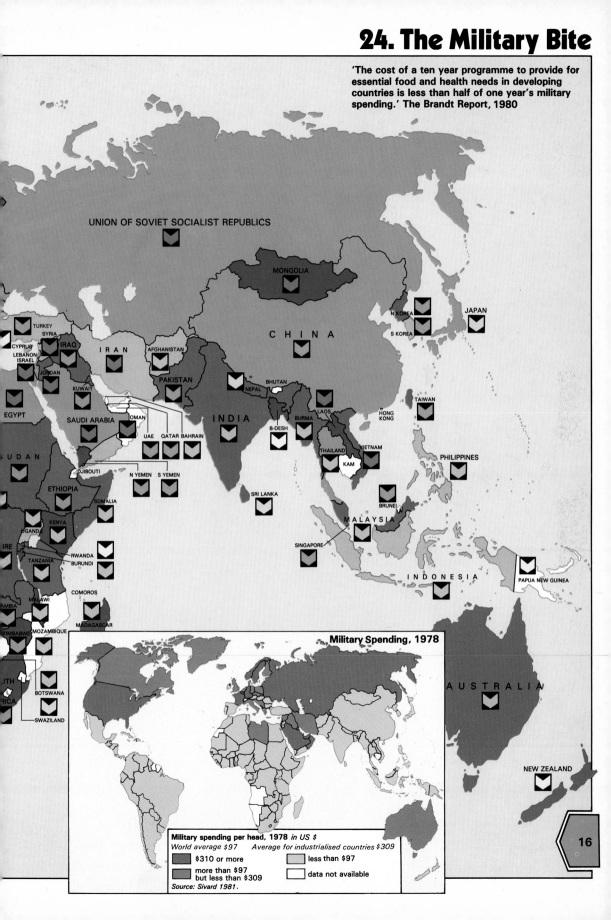

UNION OF SOVIET SOCIALIST REPUBLICS

MONGOLIA

CHINA

N KOREA

S KOREA

JAPAN

TURKEY

SYRIA

CYPRUS

LEBANON

ISRAEL

IRAQ

IRAN

AFGHANISTAN

JORDAN

KUWAIT

PAKISTAN

NEPAL

BHUTAN

TAIWAN

EGYPT

SAUDI ARABIA

OMAN

UAE

QATAR BAHRAIN

INDIA

BURMA

LAOS

HONG KONG

B-DESH

VIETNAM

SUDAN

DJIBOUTI

N YEMEN S YEMEN

THAILAND

KAM

PHILIPPINES

ETHIOPIA

SOMALIA

SRI LANKA

BRUNEI

IRE

UGANDA

KENYA

TANZANIA

RWANDA

BURUNDI

MALAYSIA

SINGAPORE

INDONESIA

PAPUA NEW GUINEA

MALAWI

COMOROS

MADAGASCAR

AMBIA

ZIMBABWE MOZAMBIQUE

AUSTRALIA

UTH

RICA

BOTSWANA

SWAZILAND

NEW ZEALAND

Military Spending, 1978

Military spending per head, 1978 *in US $*

World average $97   *Average for industrialised countries $309*

- $310 or more
- more than $97 but less than $309
- less than $97
- data not available

Source: Sivard 1981.

16

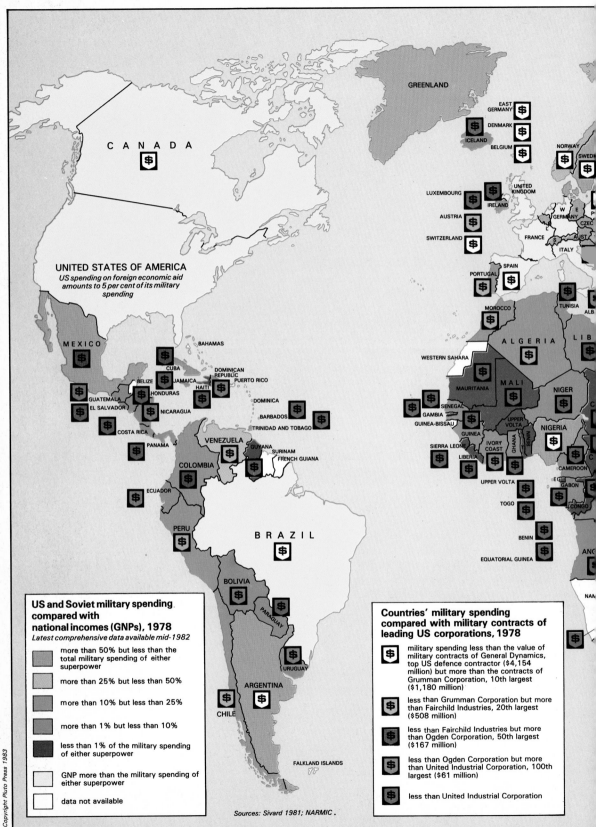

GREENLAND

CANADA

EAST GERMANY
DENMARK
ICELAND
BELGIUM
NORWAY
SWED

LUXEMBOURG
IRELAND
UNITED KINGDOM
AUSTRIA
SWITZERLAND
W GERMANY E
CZEC
FRANCE
AUST
ITALY

SPAIN
PORTUGAL

UNITED STATES OF AMERICA
US spending on foreign economic aid amounts to 5 per cent of its military spending

MOROCCO
TUNISIA
ALB

WESTERN SAHARA
ALGERIA
LIB

MEXICO
BAHAMAS

CUBA
BELIZE
JAMAICA
HAITI
DOMINICAN REPUBLIC
PUERTO RICO
GUATEMALA
HONDURAS
EL SALVADOR
NICARAGUA
COSTA RICA
DOMINICA
BARBADOS
TRINIDAD AND TOBAGO

MAURITANIA
MALI
NIGER
SENEGAL
GAMBIA
GUINEA-BISSAU
GUINEA
UPPER VOLTA
NIGERIA
SIERRA LEONE
IVORY COAST
GHANA
BENIN
LIBERIA
CAMEROON
UPPER VOLTA
EG
GABON
TOGO
CONGO
BENIN
ANG
EQUATORIAL GUINEA

PANAMA
VENEZUELA
COLOMBIA
GUYANA
SURINAM
FRENCH GUIANA
ECUADOR
PERU

BRAZIL

BOLIVIA
PARAGUAY

NAM

US and Soviet military spending compared with national incomes (GNPs), 1978

Latest comprehensive data available mid-1982

- more than 50% but less than the total military spending of either superpower
- more than 25% but less than 50%
- more than 10% but less than 25%
- more than 1% but less than 10%
- less than 1% of the military spending of either superpower
- GNP more than the military spending of either superpower
- data not available

URUGUAY
ARGENTINA
CHILE

FALKLAND ISLANDS

Countries' military spending compared with military contracts of leading US corporations, 1978

- $ military spending less than the value of military contracts of General Dynamics, top US defence contractor ($4,154 million) but more than the contracts of Grumman Corporation, 10th largest ($1,180 million)
- $ less than Grumman Corporation but more than Fairchild Industries, 20th largest ($508 million)
- $ less than Fairchild Industries but more than Ogden Corporation, 50th largest ($167 million)
- $ less than Ogden Corporation but more than United Industrial Corporation, 100th largest ($61 million)
- $ less than United Industrial Corporation

Sources: Sivard 1981; NARMIC .

Each superpower spends more on its armed forces than the combined national incomes of the 62 countries at the bottom of the world league table of GNPs.

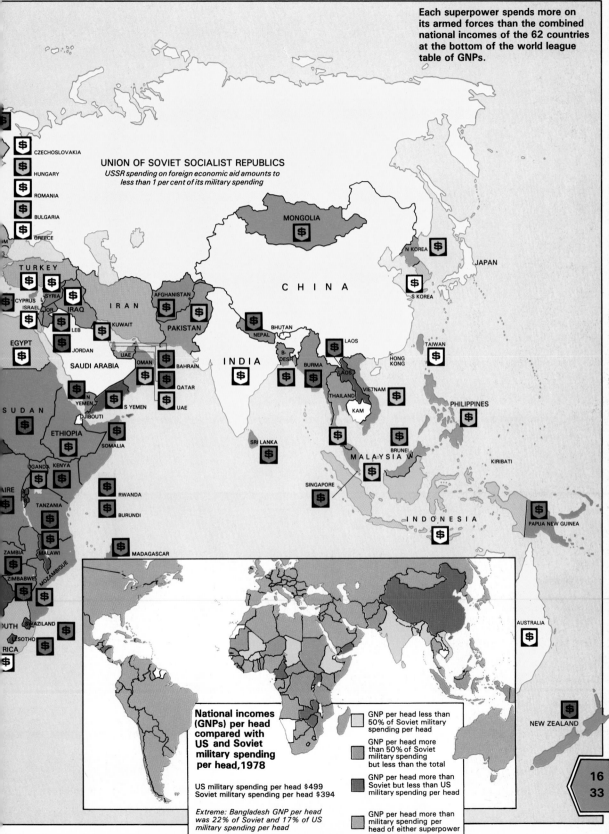

UNION OF SOVIET SOCIALIST REPUBLICS
USSR spending on foreign economic aid amounts to less than 1 per cent of its military spending

National incomes (GNPs) per head compared with US and Soviet military spending per head,1978

US military spending per head $499
Soviet military spending per head $394

Extreme: Bangladesh GNP per head was 22% of Soviet and 17% of US military spending per head

GNP per head less than 50% of Soviet military spending per head

GNP per head more than 50% of Soviet military spending but less than the total

GNP per head more than Soviet but less than US military spending per head

GNP per head more than military spending per head of either superpower

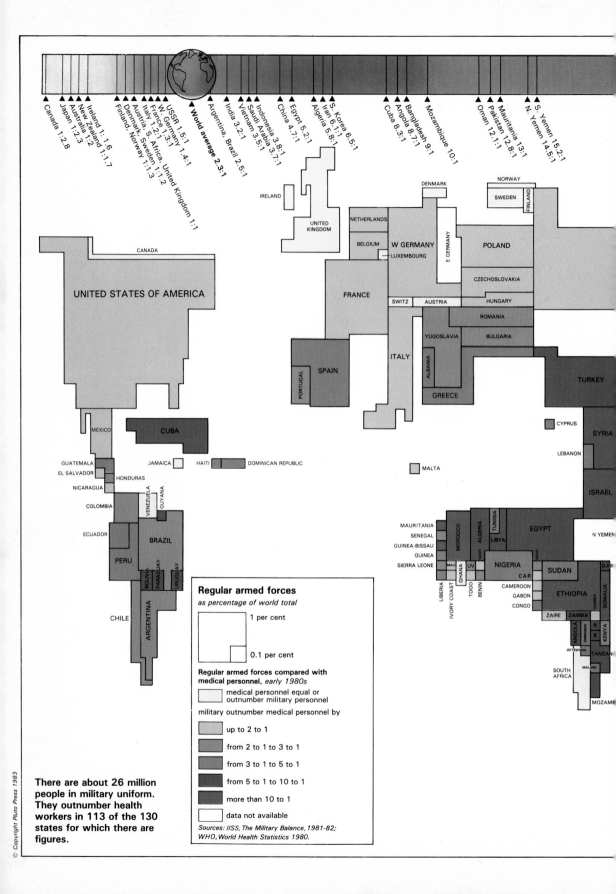

Canada 1:2.8
Japan 1:2.3
Australia 1:2.3
New Zealand 1:1.7
Ireland 1:1.6
USSR 1.5:1
W. Germany 1.4:1
France 1.2:1
Italy, S. Africa, United Kingdom 1:1
Denmark, Sweden 1:1.2
Austria, Sweden 1:1.2
Finland, Norway 1:1.3
World average 2.3:1
Argentina, Brazil 2.5:1
India 3.2:1
Vietnam 3.5:1
Saudi Arabia 3.7:1
Indonesia 3.8:1
China 4.7:1
Egypt 5.2:1
Iran 6:1
S. Korea 6.5:1
Algeria 5.8:1
Cuba 8.3:1
Angola 8.7:1
Bangladesh 9:1
Mozambique 10:1
Oman 12.1:1
Pakistan 12.8:1
Mauritania 13:1
N. Yemen 14.5:1
S. Yemen 15.2:1

Regular armed forces
as percentage of world total

1 per cent

0.1 per cent

Regular armed forces compared with medical personnel, *early 1980s*

medical personnel equal or outnumber military personnel

military outnumber medical personnel by

up to 2 to 1

from 2 to 1 to 3 to 1

from 3 to 1 to 5 to 1

from 5 to 1 to 10 to 1

more than 10 to 1

data not available

Sources: IISS, The Military Balance, 1981-82; WHO, World Health Statistics 1980.

There are about 26 million people in military uniform. They outnumber health workers in 113 of the 130 states for which there are figures.

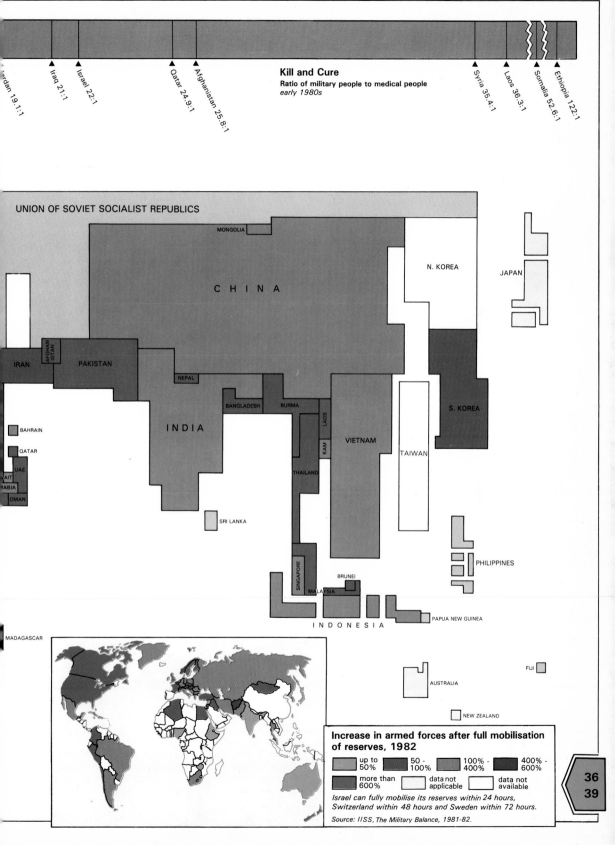

Kill and Cure
Ratio of military people to medical people
early 1980s

...rdan 19.1:1
Iraq 21:1
Israel 22:1
Qatar 24.9:1
Afghanistan 25.8:1
Syria 35.4:1
Laos 36.3:1
Somalia 52.6:1
Ethiopia 122:1

UNION OF SOVIET SOCIALIST REPUBLICS

MONGOLIA
N. KOREA
JAPAN
CHINA
IRAN
AFGHANISTAN
PAKISTAN
NEPAL
BANGLADESH
BURMA
LAOS
S. KOREA
BAHRAIN
INDIA
QATAR
UAE
KAM
VIETNAM
TAIWAN
...AIT
...ABIA
OMAN
THAILAND
SRI LANKA
SINGAPORE
BRUNEI
MALAYSIA
PHILIPPINES
PAPUA NEW GUINEA
INDONESIA
MADAGASCAR
FIJI
AUSTRALIA
NEW ZEALAND

**Increase in armed forces after full mobilisation
of reserves, 1982**

up to 50%	50 - 100%	100% - 400%	400% - 600%
more than 600%	data not applicable	data not available

*Israel can fully mobilise its reserves within 24 hours,
Switzerland within 48 hours and Sweden within 72 hours.*

Source: IISS, The Military Balance, 1981-82.

36
39

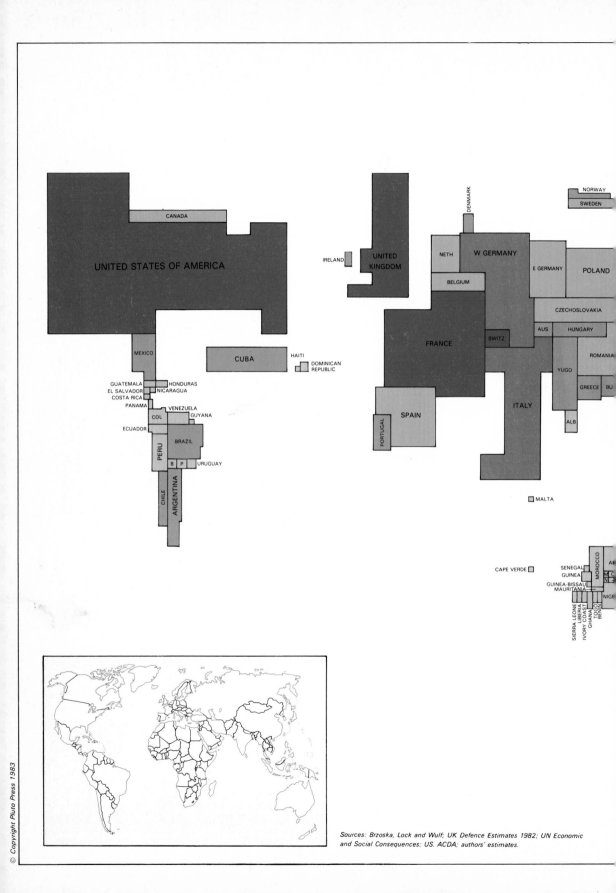

CANADA

UNITED STATES OF AMERICA

IRELAND

UNITED KINGDOM

DENMARK

NORWAY

SWEDEN

NETH

W GERMANY

E GERMANY

POLAND

BELGIUM

CZECHOSLOVAKIA

FRANCE

SWITZ

AUS

HUNGARY

MEXICO

CUBA

HAITI

DOMINICAN REPUBLIC

ROMANIA

YUGO

GUATEMALA

HONDURAS

EL SALVADOR

NICARAGUA

COSTA RICA

PANAMA

VENEZUELA

GUYANA

COL

ECUADOR

PERU

BRAZIL

B

P

URUGUAY

CHILE

ARGENTINA

GREECE

BU

ITALY

ALB

PORTUGAL

SPAIN

MALTA

CAPE VERDE

SENEGAL

GUINEA

GUINEA-BISSAU

MAURITANIA

MOROCCO

A

M

O

N

NIG

SIERRA LEONE

LIBERIA

IVORY COAST

GHANA

TOGO

BENIN

Sources: Brzoska, Lock and Wulf; UK Defence Estimates 1982; UN Economic and Social Consequences; US. ACDA; authors' estimates.

Twice as many people work for the armed forces as work within them.

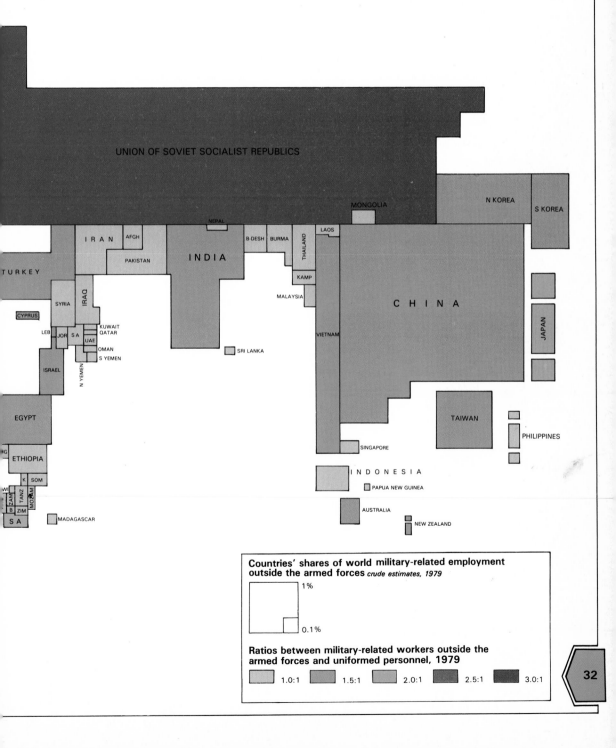

UNION OF SOVIET SOCIALIST REPUBLICS

MONGOLIA

N KOREA

S KOREA

NEPAL

IRAN

AFGH

B-DESH

BURMA

LAOS

TURKEY

PAKISTAN

INDIA

THAILAND

SYRIA

IRAQ

KAMP

MALAYSIA

C H I N A

CYPRUS

LEB

JOR

S A

KUWAIT

QATAR

UAE

OMAN

VIETNAM

JAPAN

ISRAEL

N YEMEN

S YEMEN

SRI LANKA

EGYPT

TAIWAN

PHILIPPINES

ETHIOPIA

K

SOM

SINGAPORE

WI

ZAM

TANZ

MOZAM

I N D O N E S I A

B

ZIM

PAPUA NEW GUINEA

S A

MADAGASCAR

AUSTRALIA

NEW ZEALAND

Countries' shares of world military-related employment outside the armed forces *crude estimates, 1979*

1%

0.1%

Ratios between military-related workers outside the armed forces and uniformed personnel, 1979

| 1.0:1 | 1.5:1 | 2.0:1 | 2.5:1 | 3.0:1 |

32

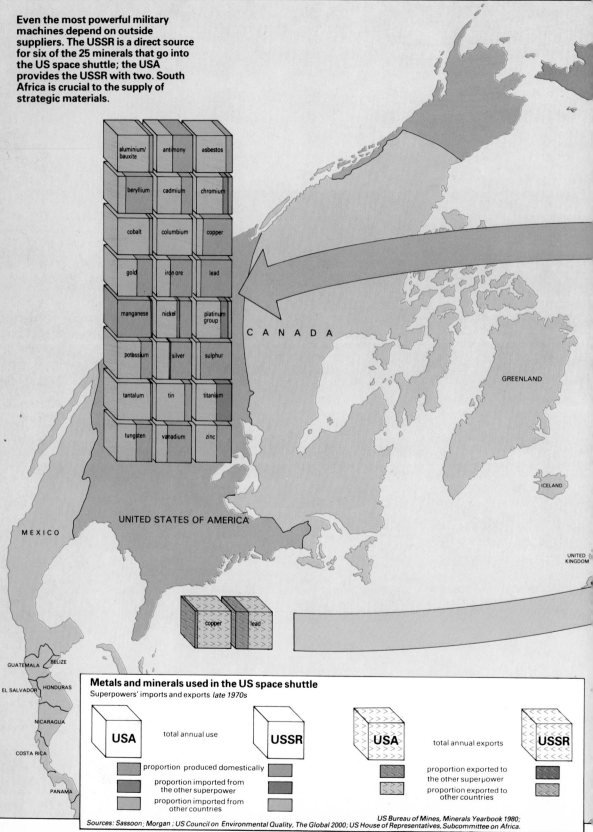

Even the most powerful military machines depend on outside suppliers. The USSR is a direct source for six of the 25 minerals that go into the US space shuttle; the USA provides the USSR with two. South Africa is crucial to the supply of strategic materials.

aluminium/bauxite | antimony | asbestos
beryllium | cadmium | chromium
cobalt | columbium | copper
gold | iron ore | lead
manganese | nickel | platinum group
potassium | silver | sulphur
tantalum | tin | titanium
tungsten | vanadium | zinc

C A N A D A

GREENLAND

ICELAND

UNITED STATES OF AMERICA

MEXICO

UNITED KINGDOM

copper | lead

GUATEMALA | BELIZE
EL SALVADOR | HONDURAS
NICARAGUA
COSTA RICA
PANAMA

Metals and minerals used in the US space shuttle
Superpowers' imports and exports *late 1970s*

USA — total annual use
USSR
USA — total annual exports
USSR

proportion produced domestically
proportion imported from the other superpower
proportion imported from other countries

proportion exported to the other superpower
proportion exported to other countries

US Bureau of Mines, Minerals Yearbook 1980;
Sources: Sassoon; Morgan; US Council on Environmental Quality, The Global 2000; US House of Representatives, Subcommittee on Africa.

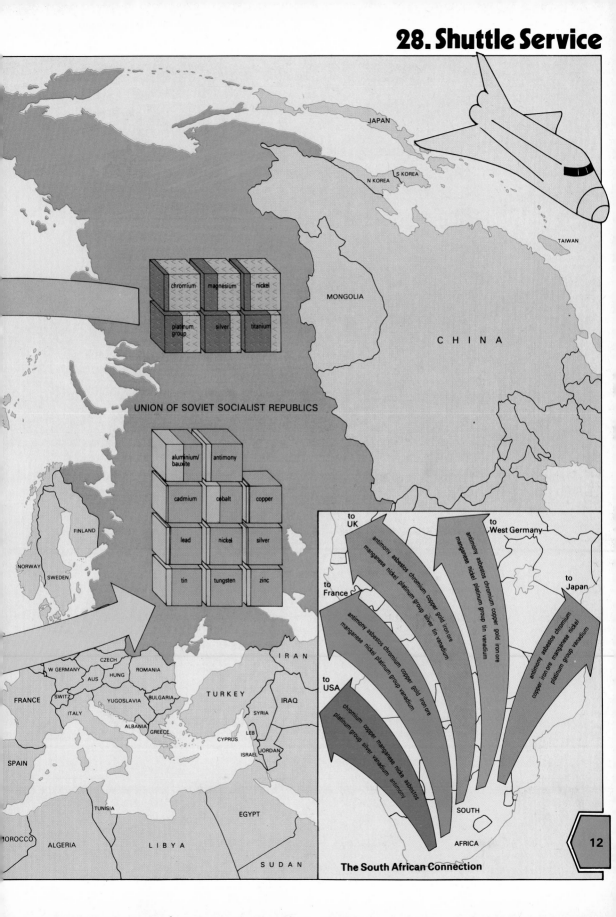

JAPAN

N KOREA   S KOREA

TAIWAN

MONGOLIA

C H I N A

| chromium | magnesium | nickel |
| platinum group | silver | titanium |

UNION OF SOVIET SOCIALIST REPUBLICS

aluminium/bauxite	antimony	
cadmium	cobalt	copper
lead	nickel	silver
tin	tungsten	zinc

FINLAND

NORWAY

SWEDEN

I R A N

CZECH
W GERMANY   ROMANIA
AUS   HUNG
SWITZ   YUGOSLAVIA   BULGARIA
FRANCE
ITALY   ALBANIA
GREECE
SPAIN

T U R K E Y   IRAQ

SYRIA
CYPRUS   LEB
ISRAEL   JORDAN

MOROCCO   ALGERIA   L I B Y A   EGYPT

TUNISIA

S U D A N

The South African Connection

to UK

antimony asbestos chromium copper gold iron ore manganese nickel platinum group silver tin vanadium

to West Germany

antimony asbestos chromium copper gold iron ore manganese nickel platinum group tin vanadium

to France

antimony asbestos chromium copper gold iron ore manganese nickel platinum group vanadium

to Japan

antimony asbestos chromium copper iron ore manganese nickel platinum group vanadium

to USA

chromium copper manganese nickel asbestos platinum group silver vanadium antimony

SOUTH

AFRICA

Part Five:
The Market Place

As the world economy slipped into recession in the 1970s, the international arms trade boomed, at least doubling in value. At the same time more states began to produce weapons and more became established arms exporters. The market grew, but also became more competitive, and with this came new interlaced patterns of power and dependence.

On the supply side of the arms trade, a few states see actual or virtual self-sufficiency in arms production as essential to their security. This policy means they must support an industry turning out ever more expensive and elaborate weapon systems. The increasing expense forces them to transfer some of the costs abroad through exports.

The major arms makers have thus come to rely on their allies and on third world states as essential additions to their home markets. Without exports, several major production lines would not be viable. This is why international arms fairs are so massive, arms corporations' brochures so lavish, the record of kickbacks and corruption so extensive. The states in the upper tiers of the international military order have come to depend on those below them. From this stems the ultimate contradiction of the arms trade, exemplified in the South Atlantic war of 1982:

when the British government went to war with Argentina, it faced an enemy largely equipped by itself and its allies.

On the demand side of the arms trade, an increasing number of states buy the appurtenances of modern military power to guarantee sovereignty and security. Their armed forces become more industry-orientated than their societies, using their growing influence to obtain greater resources. Such states become dependent on military technologies they cannot reproduce and increasingly reliant on the major arms suppliers.

For many states, the way out of this tangle is to manufacture arms themselves. But if they do no more than manufacture them, they remain dependent on external sources for their designs. Indeed, this turns out to be a greater dependence than before, since they have now committed more industrial resources to their military effort. The intricacies of power are such that, if they go further, to establish autonomous design capacities for at least some weapons, they become more enmeshed in the international military order. For to cover the enormous costs involved, they must sell their products on the international market, competing for orders on terms set by the most powerful in the business.

The first four maps in this section show the geography of the production, export and import of arms. They reveal again the starkness of the hierarchy in the international military order. They also show its potential instability in the spread of arms production and appearance of new arms exporters. As commercial competition intensifies the major exporters find that they must sell not only hardware, but also knowledge. The network of licences and agreements for producing weapons of foreign design is shown in *Map 33: Sharing the Spoils*. Collaborative design projects indicate the response of major powers to the economic burdens of military-industrial self-sufficiency. Ironically, for rich and poor states alike, a policy based on assumptions of independence and sovereignty leads inexorably into a network of interdependence.

When arms are big business, wars become a way of displaying wares. They become real-life testing grounds. Each war is closely examined, not only for its tactical and strategic lessons but also for hints on market opportunities. It is merely good business practice for the British Ministry of Defence to arrange 'Floater 83', a floating exhibition of military equipment, hoping that the label 'proved in the Falklands' will help to increase arms sales in the Middle East. *Map 34: War Fair* looks at the South Atlantic war through the eyes of industrialists and importers, eyes which see little besides the equations of cost effectiveness. A cynic might be tempted to believe that war is becoming the pursuit of commerce by other means.

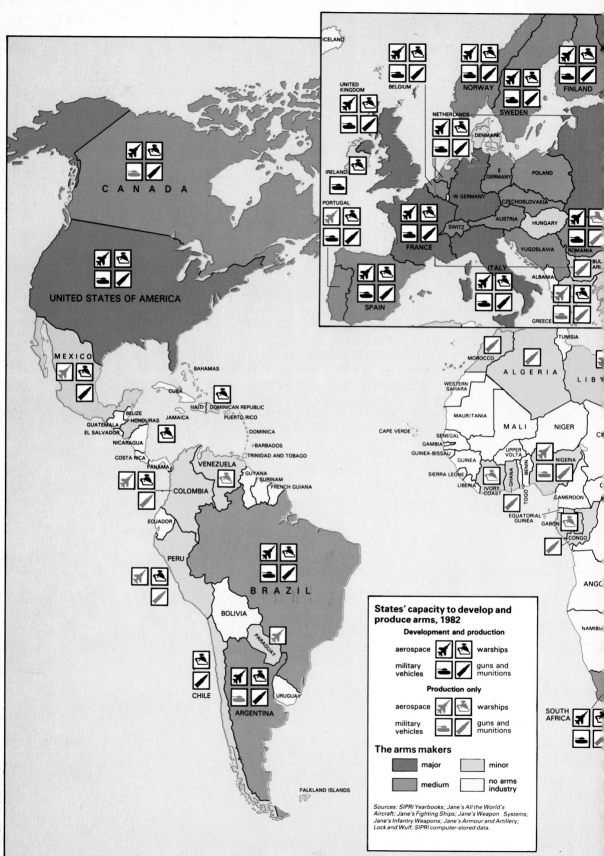

ICELAND

UNITED
KINGDOM

BELGIUM

NORWAY

SWEDEN

FINLAND

NETHERLANDS

DENMARK

IRELAND

E
GERMANY

POLAND

W GERMANY

PORTUGAL

CZECHOSLOVAKIA

SWITZ

AUSTRIA

HUNGARY

FRANCE

YUGOSLAVIA

ROMANIA

ITALY

ALBANIA

BUL
ARI

SPAIN

GREECE

CANADA

UNITED STATES OF AMERICA

MEXICO

BAHAMAS

CUBA

BELIZE
HONDURAS
GUATEMALA
EL SALVADOR
NICARAGUA
COSTA RICA
PANAMA

JAMAICA

HAITI

DOMINICAN REPUBLIC

PUERTO RICO

DOMINICA

BARBADOS

TRINIDAD AND TOBAGO

VENEZUELA

GUYANA
SURINAM
FRENCH GUIANA

COLOMBIA

ECUADOR

PERU

BRAZIL

BOLIVIA

PARAGUAY

CHILE

URUGUAY

ARGENTINA

FALKLAND ISLANDS

TUNISIA

MOROCCO

ALGERIA

LIBY

WESTERN
SAHARA

MAURITANIA

MALI

NIGER

CH

CAPE VERDE

SENEGAL
GAMBIA
GUINEA-BISSAU

UPPER
VOLTA

GUINEA

SIERRA LEONE
LIBERIA

IVORY
COAST

GHANA

BENIN

TOGO

NIGERIA

CAMEROON

EQUATORIAL
GUINEA

GABON

CONGO

ANGO

NAMIBIA

SOUTH
AFRICA

States' capacity to develop and produce arms, 1982

Development and production

aerospace   warships

military
vehicles   guns and
munitions

Production only

aerospace   warships

military
vehicles   guns and
munitions

The arms makers

major

minor

medium

no arms
industry

Sources: SIPRI Yearbooks; Jane's All the World's
Aircraft; Jane's Fighting Ships; Jane's Weapon Systems;
Jane's Infantry Weapons; Jane's Armour and Artillery;
Lock and Wulf; SIPRI computer-stored data.

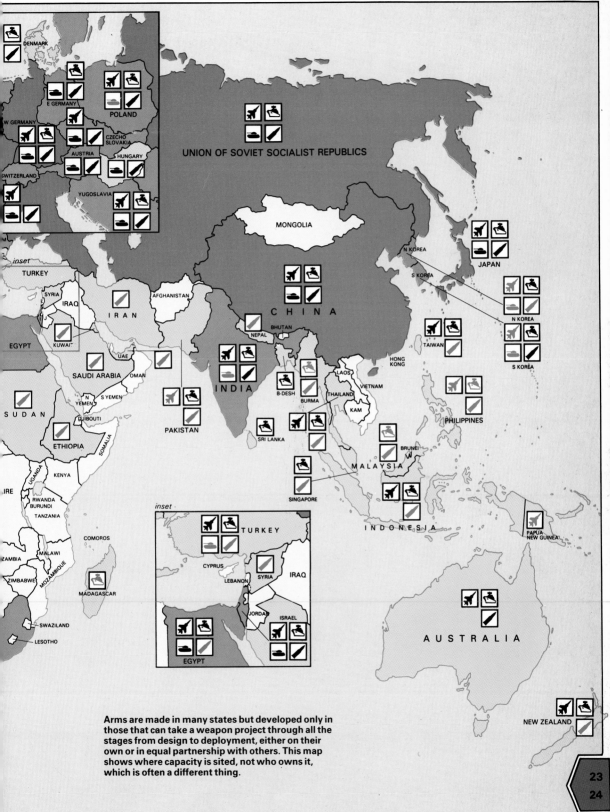

Arms are made in many states but developed only in those that can take a weapon project through all the stages from design to deployment, either on their own or in equal partnership with others. This map shows where capacity is sited, not who owns it, which is often a different thing.

23
24

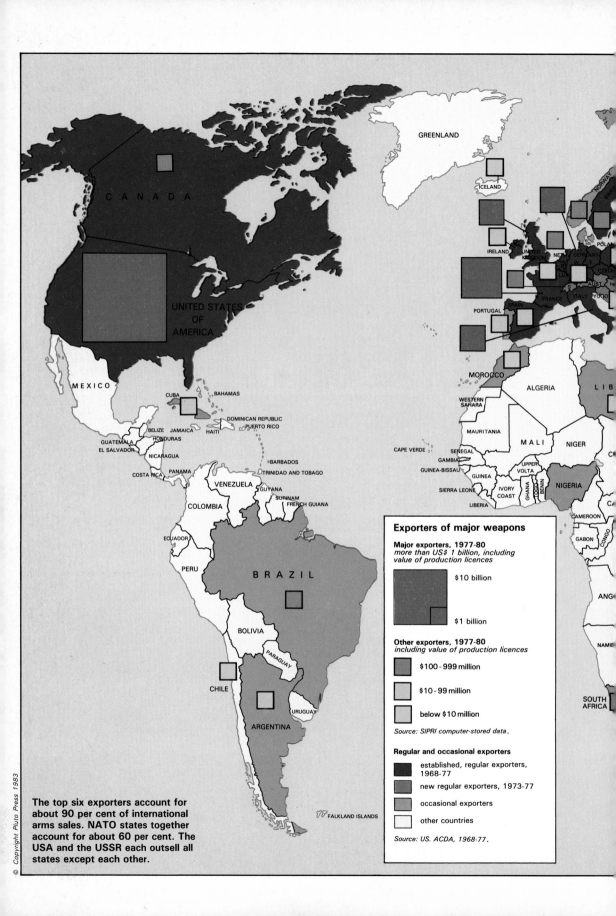

GREENLAND

ICELAND

IRELAND

NORWAY

SWE

UNITED
KINGDOM

NET

GERMANY
W E

POL

PORTUGAL

SPAIN

LUX

B

AUST

S

FRANCE

CZECH

H

ITALY

YUGO

CANADA

UNITED STATES
OF
AMERICA

MEXICO

CUBA

BAHAMAS

MOROCCO

ALGERIA

LIB

WESTERN
SAHARA

DOMINICAN REPUBLIC
PUERTO RICO

BELIZE

JAMAICA

HAITI

HONDURAS

GUATEMALA
EL SALVADOR

NICARAGUA

COSTA RICA

PANAMA

BARBADOS

TRINIDAD AND TOBAGO

VENEZUELA

GUYANA

COLOMBIA

SURINAM

FRENCH GUIANA

ECUADOR

PERU

BRAZIL

BOLIVIA

PARAGUAY

CHILE

URUGUAY

ARGENTINA

FALKLAND ISLANDS

MAURITANIA

MALI

NIGER

CAPE VERDE

SENEGAL

GAMBIA

GUINEA-BISSAU

GUINEA

SIERRA LEONE

LIBERIA

IVORY
COAST

UPPER
VOLTA

GHANA

BENIN

NIGERIA

C

CAMEROON

GABON

CONGO

CA

ANG

NAMIB

SOUTH
AFRICA

Exporters of major weapons

Major exporters, 1977-80
*more than US$ 1 billion, including
value of production licences*

$10 billion

$1 billion

Other exporters, 1977-80
including value of production licences

$100 - 999 million

$10 - 99 million

below $10 million

Source: SIPRI computer-stored data.

Regular and occasional exporters

established, regular exporters,
1968-77

new regular exporters, 1973-77

occasional exporters

other countries

Source: US. ACDA, 1968-77.

**The top six exporters account for
about 90 per cent of international
arms sales. NATO states together
account for about 60 per cent. The
USA and the USSR each outsell all
states except each other.**

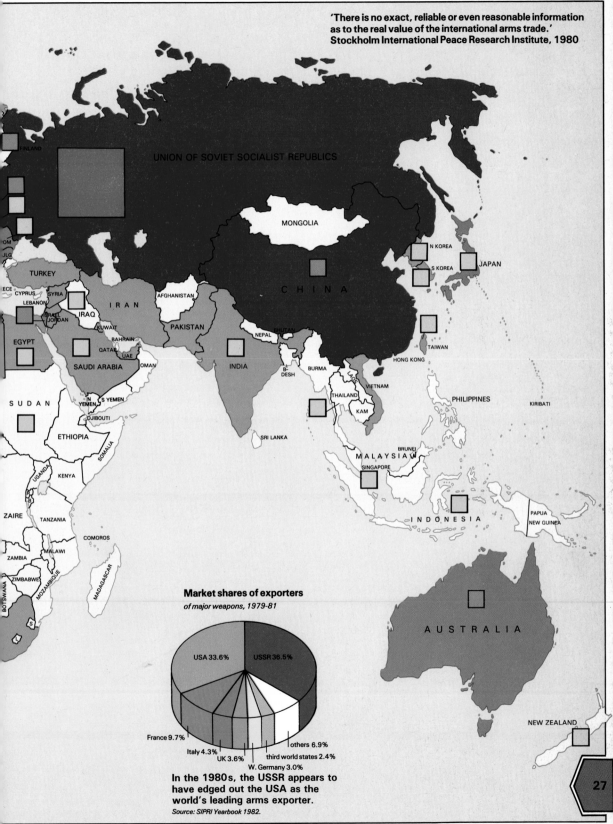

'There is no exact, reliable or even reasonable information as to the real value of the international arms trade.'
Stockholm International Peace Research Institute, 1980

FINLAND

UNION OF SOVIET SOCIALIST REPUBLICS

OM
JLG

TURKEY

MONGOLIA

N KOREA

S KOREA   JAPAN

ECE
CYPRUS   SYRIA
LEBANON
ISRAEL
JORDAN   IRAQ   IRAN   AFGHANISTAN

KUWAIT
BAHRAIN
QATAR   PAKISTAN
UAE
OMAN

EGYPT

SAUDI ARABIA   INDIA

NEPAL   BHUTAN

B-
DESH   BURMA

C H I N A

TAIWAN

HONG KONG

VIETNAM

PHILIPPINES

KIRIBATI

SUDAN

N
YEMEN   S YEMEN

DJIBOUTI

ETHIOPIA

SOMALIA

THAILAND

KAM

UGANDA

KENYA

ZAIRE

TANZANIA

COMOROS

ZAMBIA

MALAWI

ZIMBABWE

MADAGASCAR

MOZAMBIQUE

BOTSWANA

SRI LANKA

MALAYSIA
SINGAPORE

BRUNEI

I N D O N E S I A

PAPUA
NEW GUINEA

A U S T R A L I A

NEW ZEALAND

Market shares of exporters
of major weapons, 1979-81

USA 33.6%   USSR 36.5%

France 9.7%

Italy 4.3%
UK 3.6%

W. Germany 3.0%

third world states 2.4%

others 6.9%

In the 1980s, the USSR appears to have edged out the USA as the world's leading arms exporter.
Source: SIPRI Yearbook 1982.

27

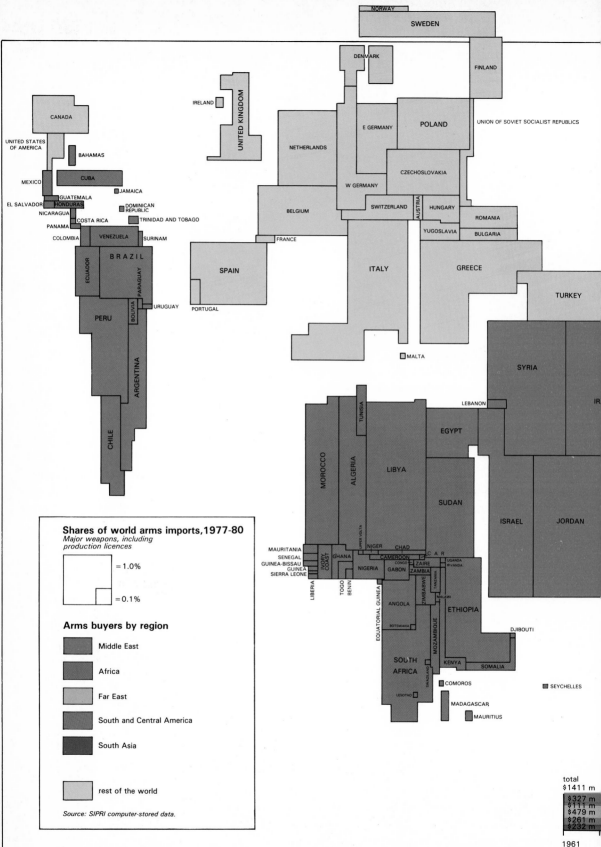

Shares of world arms imports, 1977–80
Major weapons, including production licences

□ = 1.0%
▫ = 0.1%

Arms buyers by region

Middle East

Africa

Far East

South and Central America

South Asia

rest of the world

Source: SIPRI computer-stored data.

total $1411 m
$327 m
$111 m
$479 m
$261 m
$232 m

1961

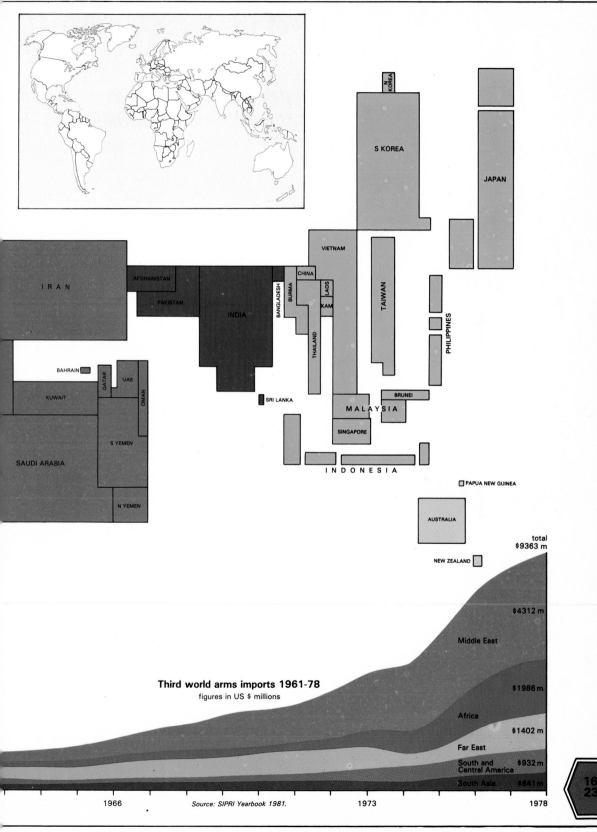

N KOREA

S KOREA

JAPAN

VIETNAM

IRAN

AFGHANISTAN

PAKISTAN

CHINA

BURMA

BANGLADESH

INDIA

LAOS

KAM

TAIWAN

THAILAND

PHILIPPINES

BAHRAIN

QATAR

UAE

OMAN

KUWAIT

SRI LANKA

BRUNEI

MALAYSIA

SINGAPORE

S YEMEN

SAUDI ARABIA

INDONESIA

N YEMEN

PAPUA NEW GUINEA

AUSTRALIA

NEW ZEALAND

total
$9363 m

$4312 m

Middle East

$1986 m

Third world arms imports 1961-78
figures in US $ millions

Africa

$1402 m

Far East

$932 m

South and
Central America

South Asia

$641 m

1966

Source: SIPRI Yearbook 1981.

1973

1978

16
23

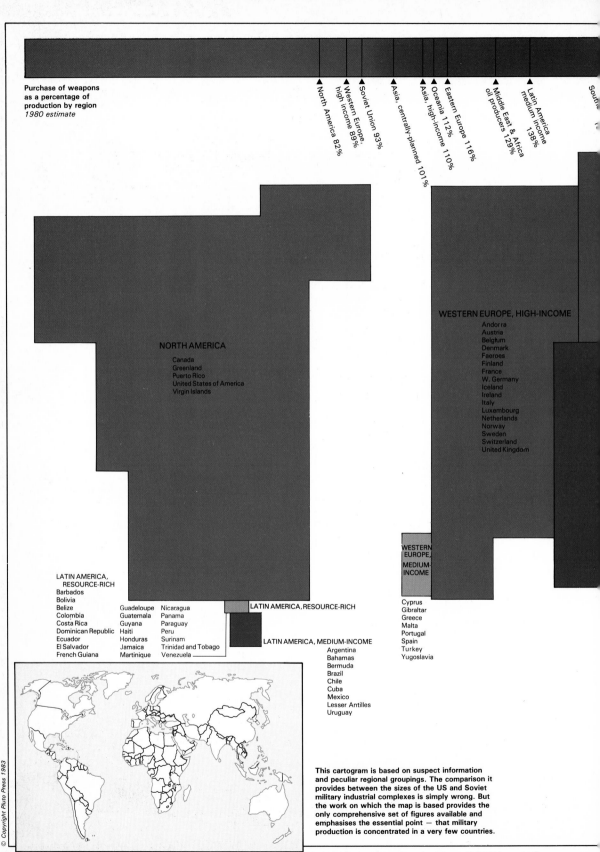

Purchase of weapons as a percentage of production by region
1980 estimate

North America 82%
Western Europe, high-income 89%
Soviet Union 93%
Asia, centrally-planned 101%
Asia, high-income 110%
Oceania 112%
Eastern Europe 116%
Middle East & Africa oil producers 129%
Latin America medium income 138%
South

NORTH AMERICA

Canada
Greenland
Puerto Rico
United States of America
Virgin Islands

WESTERN EUROPE, HIGH-INCOME

Andorra
Austria
Belgium
Denmark
Faeroes
Finland
France
W. Germany
Iceland
Ireland
Italy
Luxembourg
Netherlands
Norway
Sweden
Switzerland
United Kingdom

WESTERN EUROPE, MEDIUM-INCOME

Cyprus
Gibraltar
Greece
Malta
Portugal
Spain
Turkey
Yugoslavia

LATIN AMERICA, RESOURCE-RICH

Barbados
Bolivia
Belize
Colombia
Costa Rica
Dominican Republic
Ecuador
El Salvador
French Guiana
Guadeloupe
Guatemala
Guyana
Haiti
Honduras
Jamaica
Martinique
Nicaragua
Panama
Paraguay
Peru
Surinam
Trinidad and Tobago
Venezuela

LATIN AMERICA, RESOURCE-RICH

LATIN AMERICA, MEDIUM-INCOME

Argentina
Bahamas
Bermuda
Brazil
Chile
Cuba
Mexico
Lesser Antilles
Uruguay

This cartogram is based on suspect information and peculiar regional groupings. The comparison it provides between the sizes of the US and Soviet military industrial complexes is simply wrong. But the work on which the map is based provides the only comprehensive set of figures available and emphasises the essential point — that military production is concentrated in a very few countries.

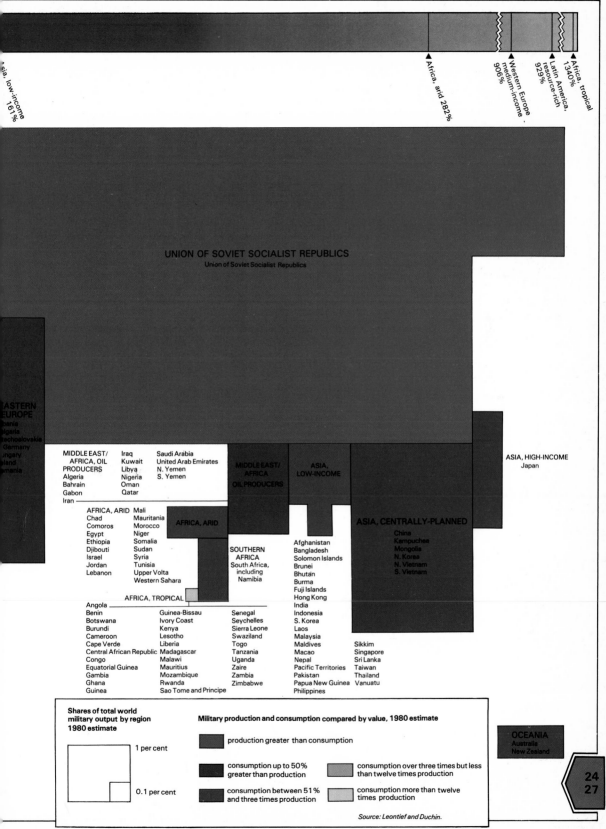

Asia, low-income 161%

Africa, arid 282%

Western Europe medium-income 906%

Latin America, resource-rich 929%

Africa, tropical 1340%

UNION OF SOVIET SOCIALIST REPUBLICS
Union of Soviet Socialist Republics

EASTERN
EUROPE
Albania
Bulgaria
Czechoslovakia
E. Germany
Hungary
Poland
Romania

MIDDLE EAST/
AFRICA, OIL
PRODUCERS
Algeria
Bahrain
Gabon
Iran

Iraq
Kuwait
Libya
Nigeria
Oman
Qatar

Saudi Arabia
United Arab Emirates
N. Yemen
S. Yemen

MIDDLE EAST/
AFRICA
OIL PRODUCERS

ASIA,
LOW-INCOME

ASIA, HIGH-INCOME
Japan

AFRICA, ARID
Chad
Comoros
Egypt
Ethiopia
Djibouti
Israel
Jordan
Lebanon

Mali
Mauritania
Morocco
Niger
Somalia
Sudan
Syria
Tunisia
Upper Volta
Western Sahara

AFRICA, ARID

SOUTHERN
AFRICA
South Africa,
including
Namibia

Afghanistan
Bangladesh
Solomon Islands
Brunei
Bhutan
Burma
Fuji Islands
Hong Kong
India
Indonesia
S. Korea
Laos
Malaysia
Maldives
Macao
Nepal
Pacific Territories
Pakistan
Papua New Guinea
Philippines

ASIA, CENTRALLY-PLANNED
China
Kampuchea
Mongolia
N. Korea
N. Vietnam
S. Vietnam

Sikkim
Singapore
Sri Lanka
Taiwan
Thailand
Vanuatu

AFRICA, TROPICAL

Angola
Benin
Botswana
Burundi
Cameroon
Cape Verde
Central African Republic
Congo
Equatorial Guinea
Gambia
Ghana
Guinea

Guinea-Bissau
Ivory Coast
Kenya
Lesotho
Liberia
Madagascar
Malawi
Mauritius
Mozambique
Rwanda
Sao Tome and Principe

Senegal
Seychelles
Sierra Leone
Swaziland
Togo
Tanzania
Uganda
Zaire
Zambia
Zimbabwe

OCEANIA
Australia
New Zealand

24
27

Shares of total world
military output by region
1980 estimate

1 per cent

0.1 per cent

Military production and consumption compared by value, 1980 estimate

production greater than consumption

consumption up to 50%
greater than production

consumption between 51%
and three times production

consumption over three times but less
than twelve times production

consumption more than twelve
times production

Source: Leontief and Duchin.

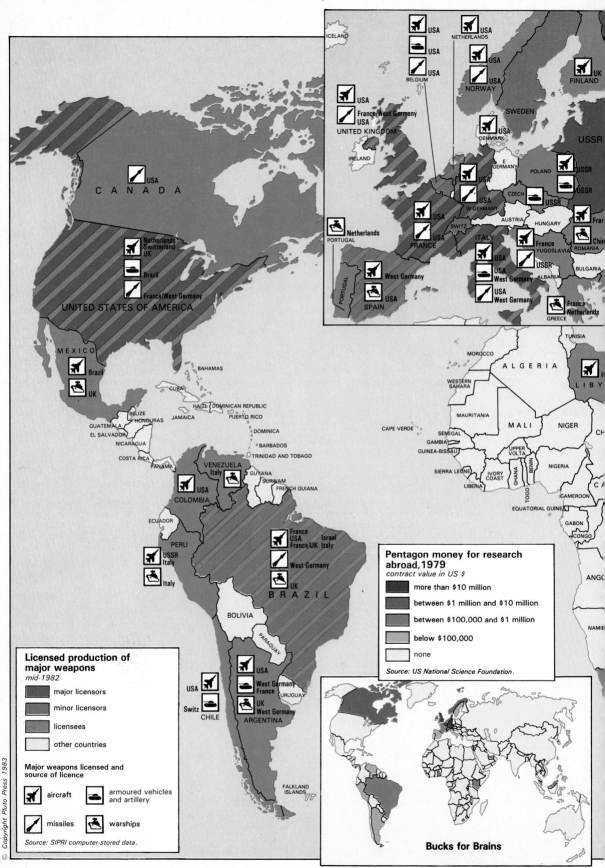

ICELAND

USA
NETHERLANDS
USA
BELGIUM
USA
NORWAY
USA
USA
UK
FINLAND

SWEDEN

USSR

USA
France/West Germany
USA
UNITED KINGDOM

IRELAND

USA
DENMARK

E.
GERMANY
POLAND
USSR
USSR

CZECH
USSR

W. GERMANY
USA
AUSTRIA
HUNGARY
Fran
USSR
Chin
ROMANIA
YUGOSLAVIA
USA
France
ITALY

BULGARIA

Netherlands
PORTUGAL

USA
FRANCE

West Germany

USA
SPAIN

CANADA

USA

Netherlands
Switzerland
UK

Brazil

France/West Germany

UNITED STATES OF AMERICA

MEXICO

Brazil

UK

BAHAMAS

CUBA

HAITI DOMINICAN REPUBLIC
JAMAICA PUERTO RICO
DOMINICA
BELIZE
GUATEMALA
HONDURAS
EL SALVADOR
NICARAGUA
BARBADOS
COSTA RICA
TRINIDAD AND TOBAGO
PANAMA

VENEZUELA
Italy
GUYANA
SURINAM
FRENCH GUIANA
USA
COLOMBIA

ECUADOR

PERU
USSR
Italy

Italy

France
USA
France/UK
Israel
Italy

West Germany

UK

B R A Z I L

BOLIVIA

PARAGUAY

USA
West Germany
France
URUGUAY
USA
UK
West Germany
CHILE
ARGENTINA

Switz

FALKLAND
ISLANDS

TUNISIA

MOROCCO
ALGERIA
LIBY

WESTERN
SAHARA

MAURITANIA
MALI
NIGER
CH

CAPE VERDE
SENEGAL
GAMBIA
GUINEA-BISSAU
UPPER
VOLTA
SIERRA LEONE
IVORY
COAST
GHANA
BENIN
NIGERIA
LIBERIA
TOGO
CAMEROON
EQUATORIAL GUINEA
GABON
CONGO

France
Netherlands
GREECE

ANGO

NAMIE

Pentagon money for research abroad, 1979
contract value in US $

- more than $10 million
- between $1 million and $10 million
- between $100,000 and $1 million
- below $100,000
- none

Source: US National Science Foundation.

Licensed production of major weapons
mid-1982

- major licensors
- minor licensors
- licensees
- other countries

Major weapons licensed and source of licence

- aircraft
- armoured vehicles and artillery
- missiles
- warships

Source: SIPRI computer-stored data.

Bucks for Brains

The international arms trade includes a trade in knowledge. Licences can be purchased for domestic production of foreign weapons; design work can be shared. In early 1982 there were 196 such products in planning or production.

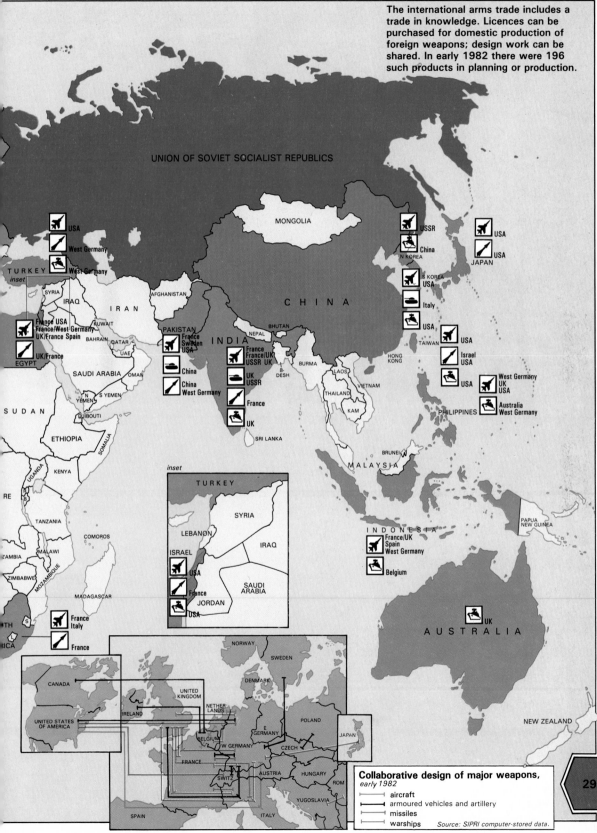

UNION OF SOVIET SOCIALIST REPUBLICS

MONGOLIA

CHINA

USA
West Germany
West Germany

TURKEY
inset

SYRIA
IRAQ
IRAN
AFGHANISTAN
KUWAIT
BAHRAIN
QATAR
UAE
OMAN

France USA
France/West Germany
UK/France Spain
UK/France
EGYPT

SAUDI ARABIA

PAKISTAN
France
Sweden
USA
China
China
West Germany

INDIA
France
France/UK
USSR UK
UK
USSR
France
UK

NEPAL
BHUTAN
B.-DESH
BURMA

SRI LANKA

USSR
China
N KOREA

S KOREA
USA

Italy

USA

TAIWAN
USA
Israel
USA

USA

USA
USA
JAPAN

LAOS
THAILAND
VIETNAM
KAM

HONG KONG

N YEMEN
S YEMEN
DJIBOUTI
ETHIOPIA
SOMALIA
SUDAN
UGANDA
KENYA

West Germany
UK
USA
Australia
West Germany

PHILIPPINES

BRUNEI

MALAYSIA

inset

TURKEY

SYRIA

LEBANON

ISRAEL

IRAQ

SAUDI ARABIA

USA
France
USA
JORDAN

INDONESIA
France/UK
Spain
West Germany
Belgium

PAPUA NEW GUINEA

COMOROS
MALAWI
MOZAMBIQUE
MADAGASCAR
TANZANIA
ZAMBIA
ZIMBABWE

France
Italy
France

AUSTRALIA
UK

NORWAY
SWEDEN
DENMARK

CANADA

UNITED KINGDOM
IRELAND
NETHER-LANDS
POLAND

UNITED STATES OF AMERICA

BELGIUM
W GERMANY
FRANCE
E GERMANY
CZECH
JAPAN

NEW ZEALAND

SWITZ
AUSTRIA
HUNGARY
ROM
YUGOSLAVIA
SPAIN
ITALY

Collaborative design of major weapons, *early 1982*

- aircraft
- armoured vehicles and artillery
- missiles
- warships

Source: SIPRI computer-stored data.

29

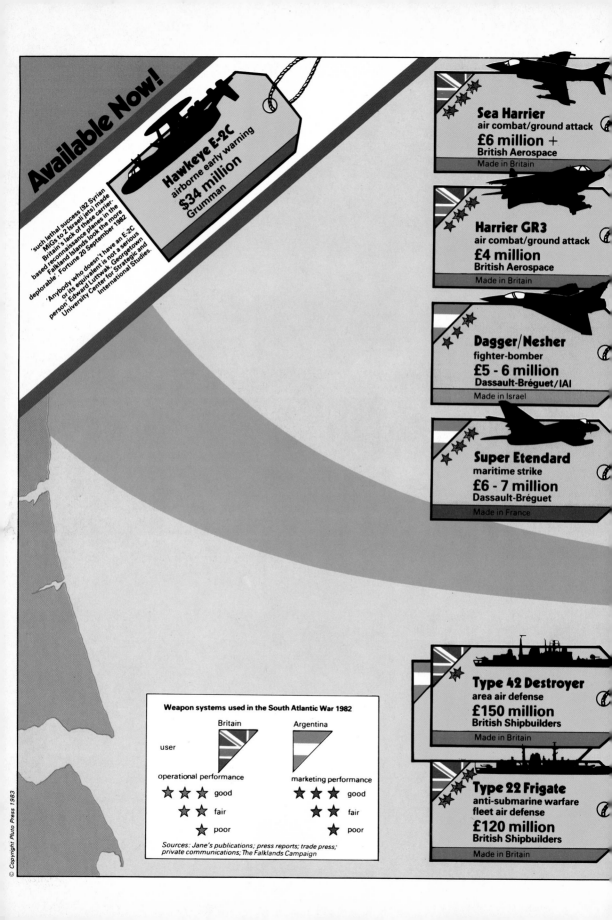

Available Now!

Hawkeye E-2C
airborne early warning
$34 million
Grumman

'such lethal success (92 Syrian MiGs to 2 Israeli jets) made Britain's lack of these carrier-based reconnaissance planes in the Falkland Islands look the more deplorable'. Fortune 20 September 1982.

'Anybody who doesn't have an E-2C or its equivalent is not a serious person' Edward Luttwak, Georgetown University Center for Strategic and International Studies.

Sea Harrier
air combat/ground attack
£6 million +
British Aerospace
Made in Britain

Harrier GR3
air combat/ground attack
£4 million
British Aerospace
Made in Britain

Dagger/Nesher
fighter-bomber
£5 - 6 million
Dassault-Bréguet/IAI
Made in Israel

Super Etendard
maritime strike
£6 - 7 million
Dassault-Bréguet
Made in France

Type 42 Destroyer
area air defense
£150 million
British Shipbuilders
Made in Britain

Type 22 Frigate
anti-submarine warfare
fleet air defense
£120 million
British Shipbuilders
Made in Britain

Weapon systems used in the South Atlantic War 1982

Britain   Argentina

user

operational performance   marketing performance

★★★ good   ★★★ good
★★ fair   ★★ fair
★ poor   ★ poor

Sources: Jane's publications; press reports; trade press; private communications; The Falklands Campaign

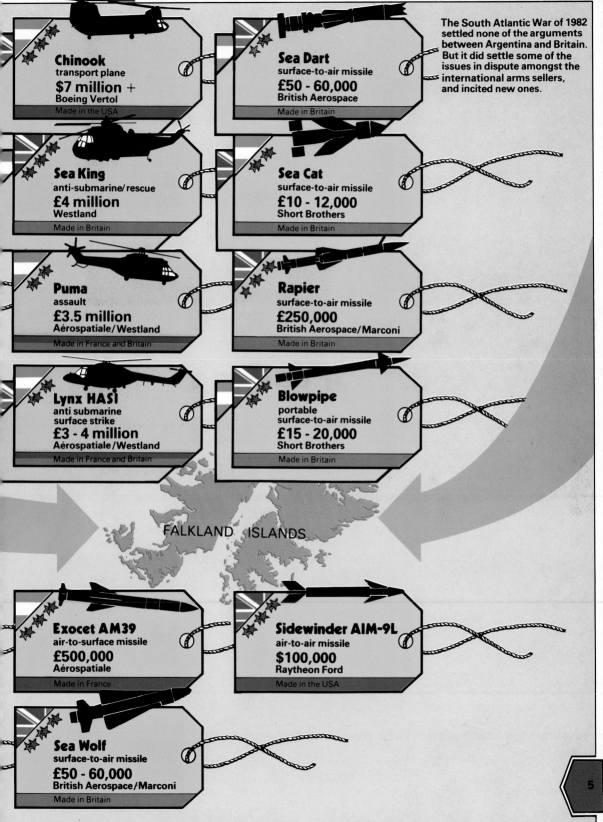

The South Atlantic War of 1982 settled none of the arguments between Argentina and Britain. But it did settle some of the issues in dispute amongst the international arms sellers, and incited new ones.

Chinook
transport plane
$7 million +
Boeing Vertol
Made in the USA

Sea Dart
surface-to-air missile
£50 - 60,000
British Aerospace
Made in Britain

Sea King
anti-submarine/rescue
£4 million
Westland
Made in Britain

Sea Cat
surface-to-air missile
£10 - 12,000
Short Brothers
Made in Britain

Puma
assault
£3.5 million
Aérospatiale/Westland
Made in France and Britain

Rapier
surface-to-air missile
£250,000
British Aerospace/Marconi
Made in Britain

Lynx HAS1
anti submarine
surface strike
£3 - 4 million
Aérospatiale/Westland
Made in France and Britain

Blowpipe
portable
surface-to-air missile
£15 - 20,000
Short Brothers
Made in Britain

FALKLAND ISLANDS

Exocet AM39
air-to-surface missile
£500,000
Aérospatiale
Made in France

Sidewinder AIM-9L
air-to-air missile
$100,000
Raytheon Ford
Made in the USA

Sea Wolf
surface-to-air missile
£50 - 60,000
British Aerospace/Marconi
Made in Britain

Part Six:
Collateral Damage

'Collateral damage' is an American military term which describes the unintended but unavoidable destruction caused by warfare. When a military target is attacked, it is only too likely that civilians will also be hurt. This may often be regretted, but is never allowed to deter the military from their task. In a larger sense, the international military order inflicts many social, political, moral and human casualties, which are widely deplored even as the policies which necessarily create them are pursued. Many of the products of this larger collateral damage are treated throughout this atlas. Further, specific, aspects are dealt with in the maps of this section.

The ultimate victim of collateral damage may be humanity itself. In the meantime, human beings and our natural and social environments are continuing victims. In much of the world, military rule is an established norm (see *Map 35: Military Rule*). Some countries where the military have ruled in the past may now have a different form of government. Yet the memory of previous domination by the armed forces restricts the range of political choice.

Military organisations have their own interests, their own conceptions of what is right and wrong, acceptable and unacceptable. Deliberately isolated in work, domicile, dress and behaviour from the society it is their ostensible function to protect, their values develop a particular authoritarian slant. With their own right to dissent from order strictly circumscribed, they tend to regard the dissent of others with impatience. Used to preparing against enemies, they tend to see enemies everywhere. To protect society from itself, they step in and systematically repress its freedoms while showing no great record of competence in economic or social management.

Of course, there are occasions when the armed forces of a country have been the instruments for overthrowing dictatorship, as in Portugal in 1974. But such incidents are, in the general run of world affairs, minor exceptions.

Absence of military rule does not mean, however, the abstention of the military from social and political affairs. All armed forces exist at least as much for purposes of domestic control as for reasons of external security. Many armed forces receive a particularly intense degree of training for this domestic role, and, as *Map 36: The Military as Police* shows, many have a wealth of experience in confronting enemies at home. The distinction beween police and military functions is all too easily lost and, with it, civil freedoms and rights. As the policing function is militarised and the military becomes practised in certain kinds of policing, so dissent is treated as if it were criminal, first in the thinking of the military and police, and later in practice.

In many countries, the social environment is a fragile compromise that permits some room for freedom, some possibility of progress. The natural environment is even more sensitive. All the major human enterprises of industrialisation and exploitation of natural resources affect the natural environment, often upsetting the intricate delicacy of the system. In the age of the international military order, war and preparations for war wreak particular havoc.

The deployment of nuclear weapons courts great risks. The dangers of accident are alarming enough in themselves, but they are even more threatening as potential triggers of nuclear holocaust. Human fallibility is revealed in *Map 37: Broken Arrows, Bent Spears*.

Armed forces have never respected the natural environment. In the name of protecting freedom and providing security, they have denied its use to others. They have destroyed it inadvertently in the course of war. They have destroyed it deliberately in order to destroy the people it supports. They have poisoned it (see *Map 38: The Martyred Earth*) in their tests of nuclear weapons.

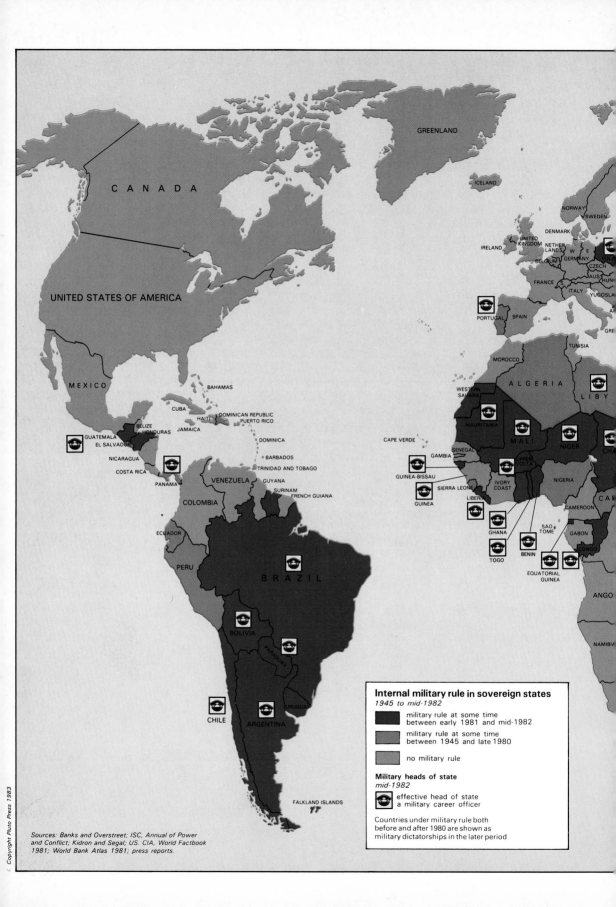

Internal military rule in sovereign states
1945 to mid-1982

- ■ military rule at some time between early 1981 and mid-1982
- ▨ military rule at some time between 1945 and late 1980
- ☐ no military rule

Military heads of state
mid-1982

effective head of state a military career officer

Countries under military rule both before and after 1980 are shown as military dictatorships in the later period

Sources: Banks and Overstreet; ISC, Annual of Power and Conflict; Kidron and Segal; US. CIA, World Factbook 1981; World Bank Atlas 1981; press reports.

© Copyright Pluto Press 1983

A quarter of the world's people know what military rule is because they or their parents have experienced it.

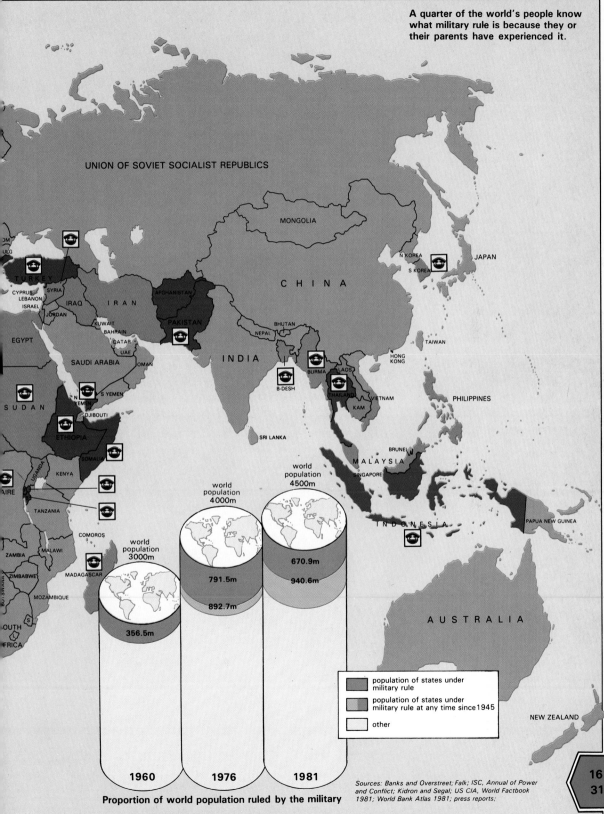

UNION OF SOVIET SOCIALIST REPUBLICS

MONGOLIA

CHINA

N KOREA

S KOREA

JAPAN

TURKEY

CYPRUS
LEBANON
ISRAEL
SYRIA

IRAQ

IRAN

AFGHANISTAN

PAKISTAN

BHUTAN

NEPAL

INDIA

BURMA

LAOS

TAIWAN

HONG KONG

VIETNAM

PHILIPPINES

JORDAN

KUWAIT

BAHRAIN

QATAR

UAE

OMAN

EGYPT

SAUDI ARABIA

N YEMEN

S YEMEN

SUDAN

DJIBOUTI

ETHIOPIA

SOMALIA

UGANDA

KENYA

ZAIRE

TANZANIA

COMOROS

ZAMBIA

MALAWI

ZIMBABWE

MOZAMBIQUE

MADAGASCAR

BOTSWANA

SOUTH AFRICA

SRI LANKA

THAILAND

KAM

MALAYSIA

SINGAPORE

BRUNEI

INDONESIA

PAPUA NEW GUINEA

AUSTRALIA

NEW ZEALAND

world population 4500m

670.9m

940.6m

world population 4000m

791.5m

892.7m

world population 3000m

356.5m

	population of states under military rule
	population of states under military rule at any time since 1945
	other

1960   **1976**   **1981**

Proportion of world population ruled by the military

Sources: Banks and Overstreet; Falk; ISC, Annual of Power and Conflict; Kidron and Segal; US CIA, World Factbook 1981; World Bank Atlas 1981; press reports;

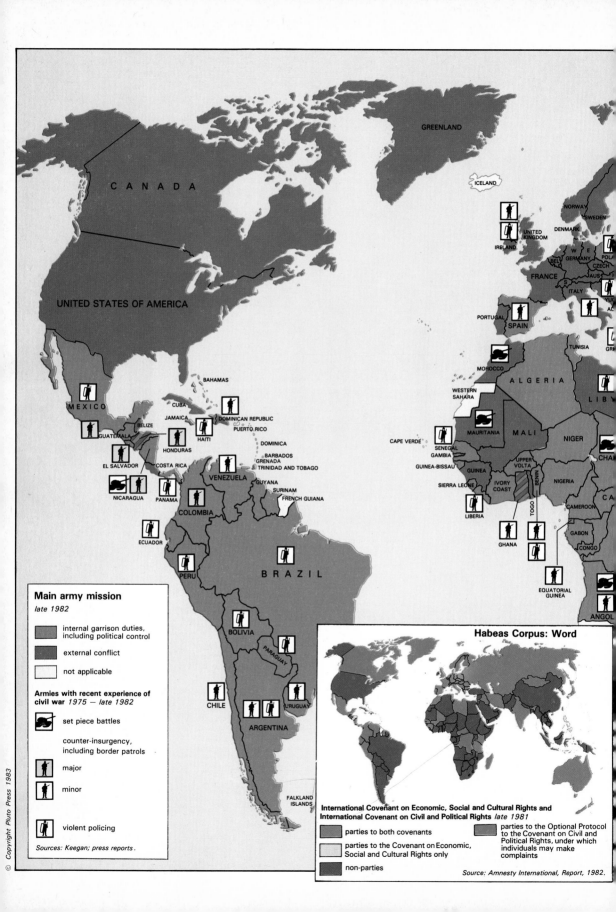

Main army mission
late 1982

internal garrison duties, including political control

external conflict

not applicable

Armies with recent experience of civil war *1975 – late 1982*

set piece battles

counter-insurgency, including border patrols

major

minor

violent policing

Sources: Keegan; press reports.

Habeas Corpus: Word

International Covenant on Economic, Social and Cultural Rights and International Covenant on Civil and Political Rights *late 1981*

parties to both covenants

parties to the Covenant on Economic, Social and Cultural Rights only

non-parties

parties to the Optional Protocol to the Covenant on Civil and Political Rights, under which individuals may make complaints

Source: Amnesty International, Report, 1982.

© Copyright Pluto Press 1983

GREENLAND

ICELAND

NORWAY

SWEDEN

DENMARK

C A N A D A

UNITED KINGDOM

IRELAND

W E GERMANY POLA
BEL CZECH

FRANCE AUS

ITALY

PORTUGAL

SPAIN

TUNISIA GR

UNITED STATES OF AMERICA

MOROCCO

A L G E R I A

LIBY

WESTERN SAHARA

BAHAMAS

CUBA

JAMAICA

BELIZE

MEXICO

GUATEMALA

HONDURAS

EL SALVADOR COSTA RICA

NICARAGUA PANAMA

DOMINICAN REPUBLIC

PUERTO RICO

HAITI

DOMINICA

BARBADOS
GRENADA
TRINIDAD AND TOBAGO

VENEZUELA

GUYANA

SURINAM

FRENCH GUIANA

COLOMBIA

ECUADOR

PERU

B R A Z I L

CAPE VERDE

MAURITANIA M A L I

NIGER

CHA

SENEGAL

GAMBIA

UPPER
VOLTA

GUINEA-BISSAU

GUINEA

SIERRA LEONE

IVORY
COAST

BENIN
TOGO

NIGERIA

CAMEROON

CA

LIBERIA

GHANA

GABON

CONGO

EQUATORIAL
GUINEA

ANGOL

BOLIVIA

PARAGUAY

CHILE

ARGENTINA

URUGUAY

FALKLAND
ISLANDS

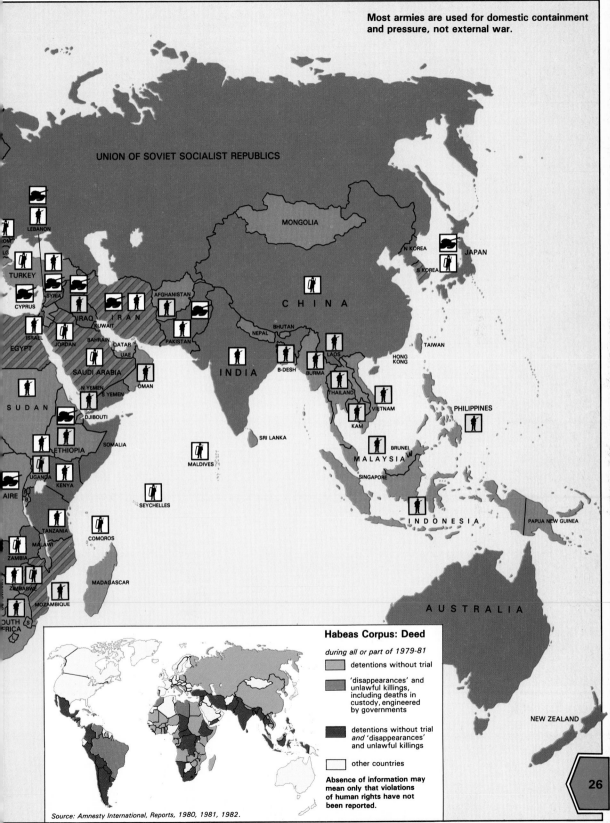

Most armies are used for domestic containment and pressure, not external war.

Habeas Corpus: Deed

during all or part of 1979-81

- detentions without trial
- 'disappearances' and unlawful killings, including deaths in custody, engineered by governments
- detentions without trial *and* 'disappearances' and unlawful killings
- other countries

Absence of information may mean only that violations of human rights have not been reported.

Source: Amnesty International, Reports, 1980, 1981, 1982.

26

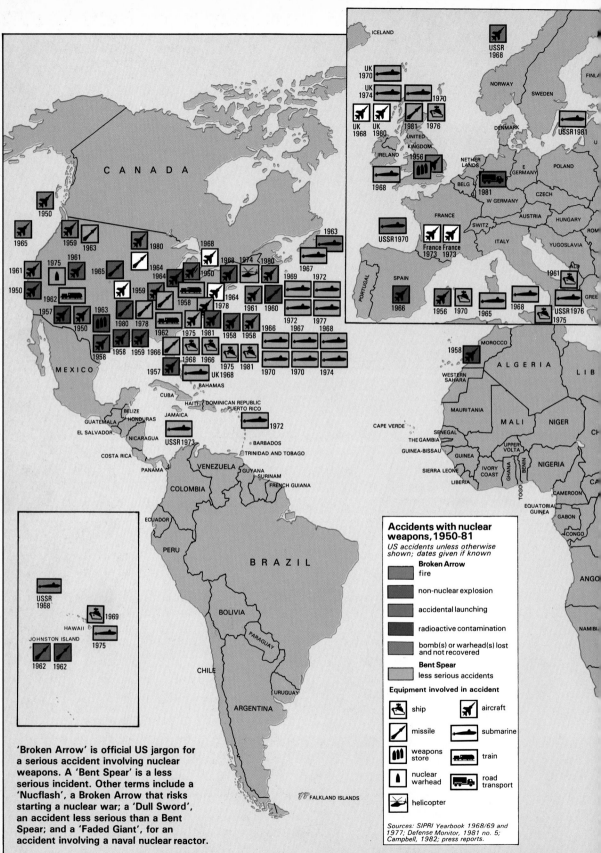

Accidents with nuclear weapons, 1950-81

US accidents unless otherwise shown; dates given if known

Broken Arrow
fire
non-nuclear explosion
accidental launching
radioactive contamination
bomb(s) or warhead(s) lost and not recovered

Bent Spear
less serious accidents

Equipment involved in accident

ship aircraft
missile submarine
weapons store train
nuclear warhead road transport
helicopter

Sources: SIPRI Yearbook 1968/69 and 1977; Defense Monitor, 1981 no. 5; Campbell, 1982; press reports.

'Broken Arrow' is official US jargon for a serious accident involving nuclear weapons. A 'Bent Spear' is a less serious incident. Other terms include a 'Nucflash', a Broken Arrow that risks starting a nuclear war; a 'Dull Sword', an accident less serious than a Bent Spear; and a 'Faded Giant', for an accident involving a naval nuclear reactor.

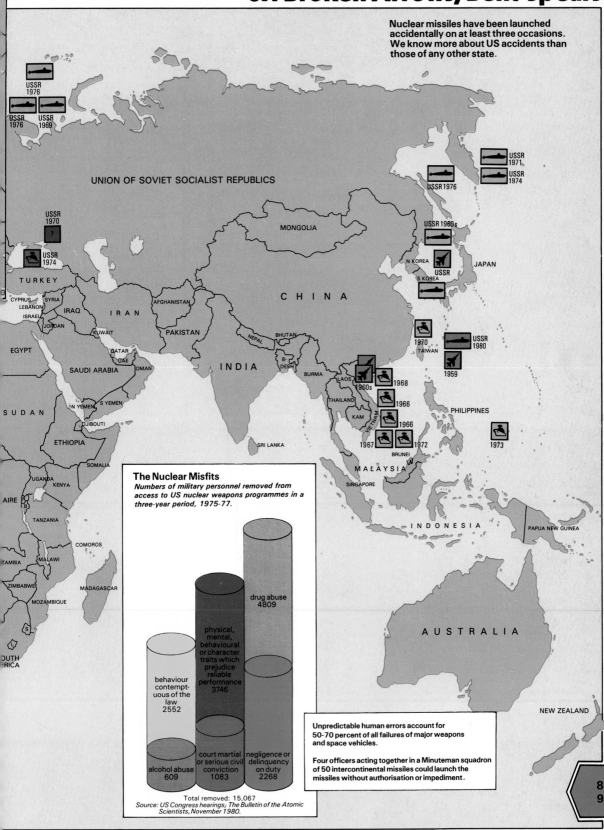

37. Broken Arrows, Bent Spears

Nuclear missiles have been launched accidentally on at least three occasions. We know more about US accidents than those of any other state.

USSR 1976

USSR 1976   USSR 1969

UNION OF SOVIET SOCIALIST REPUBLICS

USSR 1971

USSR 1974

USSR 1976

USSR 1960s

USSR 1970

USSR 1974

TURKEY

USSR 1970

MONGOLIA

JAPAN

N KOREA

S KOREA   USSR

CYPRUS   SYRIA

LEBANON   IRAQ   IRAN

ISRAEL

JORDAN   KUWAIT   AFGHANISTAN

EGYPT   QATAR   PAKISTAN

SAUDI ARABIA   UAE   OMAN

C H I N A

NEPAL   BHUTAN

B-DESH   BURMA

I N D I A

TAIWAN   USSR 1980

1970

1959

N YEMEN   S YEMEN

DJIBOUTI

SUDAN   LAOS

1960s   1968

ETHIOPIA   THAILAND   1966

SRI LANKA   KAM   1966   PHILIPPINES

SOMALIA   VIETNAM

UGANDA   KENYA   1967   1972   1973

AIRE   BRUNEI

TANZANIA   MALAYSIA

COMOROS   SINGAPORE

The Nuclear Misfits

Numbers of military personnel removed from access to US nuclear weapons programmes in a three-year period, 1975-77.

ZAMBIA   MALAWI

ZIMBABWE   MADAGASCAR

MOZAMBIQUE   I N D O N E S I A   PAPUA NEW GUINEA

drug abuse
4809

physical,
mental,
behavioural
or character
traits which
prejudice
reliable
performance
3746

behaviour
contempt-
uous of the
law
2552

A U S T R A L I A

alcohol abuse
609

court martial
or serious civil
conviction
1083

negligence or
delinquency
on duty
2268

NEW ZEALAND

Unpredictable human errors account for 50-70 percent of all failures of major weapons and space vehicles.

Four officers acting together in a Minuteman squadron of 50 intercontinental missiles could launch the missiles without authorisation or impediment.

Total removed: 15,067
Source: US Congress hearings; The Bulletin of the Atomic Scientists, November 1980.

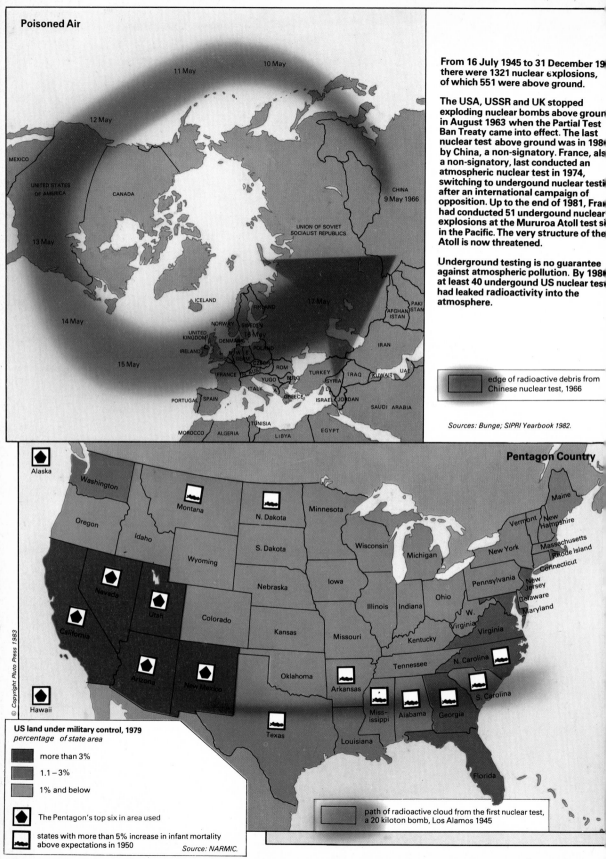

Poisoned Air

11 May
10 May
12 May
MEXICO
UNITED STATES OF AMERICA
CANADA
CHINA
9 May 1966
13 May
UNION OF SOVIET SOCIALIST REPUBLICS
14 May
ICELAND
NORWAY
SWEDEN
FINLAND
17 May
AFGHAN-ISTAN
PAKI-STAN
15 May
UNITED KINGDOM
IRELAND
DENMARK
16 May
N'W'LE'S
B'G'M
GER'MY
CZECH
AUS
POLAND
IRAN
FRANCE
SLI
YUGO
ROM
BULG
TURKEY
IRAQ
KUWAIT
UAE
ITALY
SYRIA
SPAIN
GREECE
ISRAEL JORDAN
SAUDI ARABIA
PORTUGAL
MOROCCO
TUNISIA
ALGERIA
LIBYA
EGYPT

From 16 July 1945 to 31 December 19
there were 1321 nuclear explosions,
of which 551 were above ground.

The USA, USSR and UK stopped
exploding nuclear bombs above groun
in August 1963 when the Partial Test
Ban Treaty came into effect. The last
nuclear test above ground was in 198
by China, a non-signatory. France, als
a non-signatory, last conducted an
atmospheric nuclear test in 1974,
switching to undergound nuclear testi
after an international campaign of
opposition. Up to the end of 1981, Fra
had conducted 51 undergound nuclear
explosions at the Mururoa Atoll test si
in the Pacific. The very structure of the
Atoll is now threatened.

Underground testing is no guarantee
against atmospheric pollution. By 198
at least 40 undergound US nuclear tes
had leaked radioactivity into the
atmosphere.

edge of radioactive debris from
Chinese nuclear test, 1966

Sources: Bunge; SIPRI Yearbook 1982.

Pentagon Country

Alaska
Washington
Montana
N. Dakota
Minnesota
Maine
Oregon
Idaho
S. Dakota
Wisconsin
Michigan
New York
Vermont
New Hampshire
Massachusetts
Rhode Island
Connecticut
Wyoming
Nevada
Utah
Colorado
Nebraska
Iowa
Illinois
Indiana
Ohio
Pennsylvania
New Jersey
Delaware
Maryland
W. Virginia
Virginia
California
Kansas
Missouri
Kentucky
Tennessee
N. Carolina
Arizona
New Mexico
Oklahoma
Arkansas
Mississippi
Alabama
Georgia
S. Carolina
Hawaii
Texas
Louisiana
Florida

© Copyright Pluto Press 1983

US land under military control, 1979
percentage of state area

more than 3%

1.1 – 3%

1% and below

The Pentagon's top six in area used

states with more than 5% increase in infant mortality
above expectations in 1950

path of radioactive cloud from the first nuclear test,
a 20 kiloton bomb, Los Alamos 1945

Source: NARMIC.

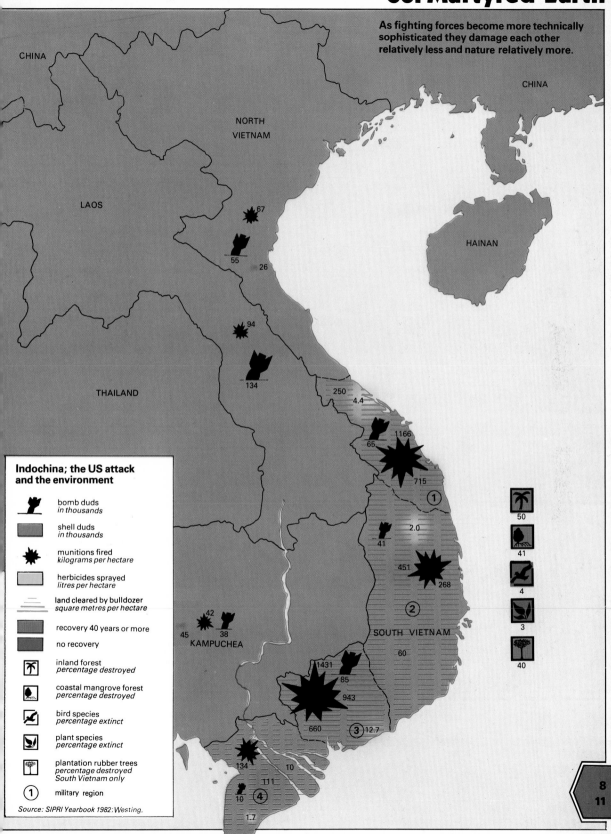

As fighting forces become more technically sophisticated they damage each other relatively less and nature relatively more.

CHINA

NORTH VIETNAM

LAOS

CHINA

HAINAN

67

55   26

94

134

THAILAND

250
4.4

65   1166

715

① 1

2.0

41

451   268

② 2

SOUTH VIETNAM

60

42

45   38

KAMPUCHEA

1431

85

943

660   ③ 12.7

134

10

111

10   ④ 4

1.7

Indochina; the US attack and the environment

bomb duds
in thousands

shell duds
in thousands

munitions fired
kilograms per hectare

herbicides sprayed
litres per hectare

land cleared by bulldozer
square metres per hectare

recovery 40 years or more

no recovery

inland forest
percentage destroyed

coastal mangrove forest
percentage destroyed

bird species
percentage extinct

plant species
percentage extinct

plantation rubber trees
*percentage destroyed
South Vietnam only*

① military region

Source: SIPRI Yearbook 1982: Westing.

50

41

4

3

40

Part Seven: Break~up?

The international military order, a hierarchy of power based on
war, the threat of war and on permanent preparations for war, is
one way of organising world affairs. It is not a productive,
generous, humane or safe way. And it is not the only way. It is
not often recognised for what it is: one of many options, created

by the powerful for their own benefit and aggrandisement.

Its current costs are high; its potential costs are beyond reckoning. It has brought us close to catastrophe, and questions whether or not human society has a future at all, let alone an attractive one.

Even at the heart of the international military order, all is not well. The growing costs of military technology are imposing intolerable strains on the most powerful of states. Stockpiling the most destructive weapons provides no sense of increased security. Economic recession and political crisis provide irritants for the management of military alliance. Many governments, even where the military rule, cannot rely on more than a small elite of the armed forces. And disaffection and demoralisation may be rampant in the forces (see *Map 39: Achilles' Heel*), even where there are no major political disagreements between the military and the government. These are circumstances which may lead to desperate and dangerous actions. But they may also provide a moment in which the military role itself is questioned, challenged, changed.

Outside the military institutions a rebellion is going on against some of the consequences of the international military order, against the distortion of priorities evidenced by high spending on the military, against the view that more weapons provide more security. Growing numbers of people see themselves, not as the fortunate beneficiaries of a great deal of protection, but as the certain victims should permanent military confrontation spill over into hot war.

The movements shown in *Map 40: A New Order?* are recent and they are fragile entrants to the political stages of their countries. They have affected public attitudes about the new weapons at the forefront of an intensified arms race and military confrontation. But they face a powerful and sophisticated opposition capable of utilising a wide range of counter-tactics. So deep is the political entrenchment of the international military order that these movements have barely begun to shift state policies.

The leading military powers cannot get us out of the historic pit which they daily deepen. If there is to be an alternative, based on a greater respect for humanity and for our natural environment, it must come from a popular movement.

Once a system has been recognised for what it is, a matter of social and political choice, alternatives can be conceived. Millions of people now understand the dangers of continuing on our present path and are glimpsing the outlines of an alternative. They have decided that something can and must be done. That is no small thing.

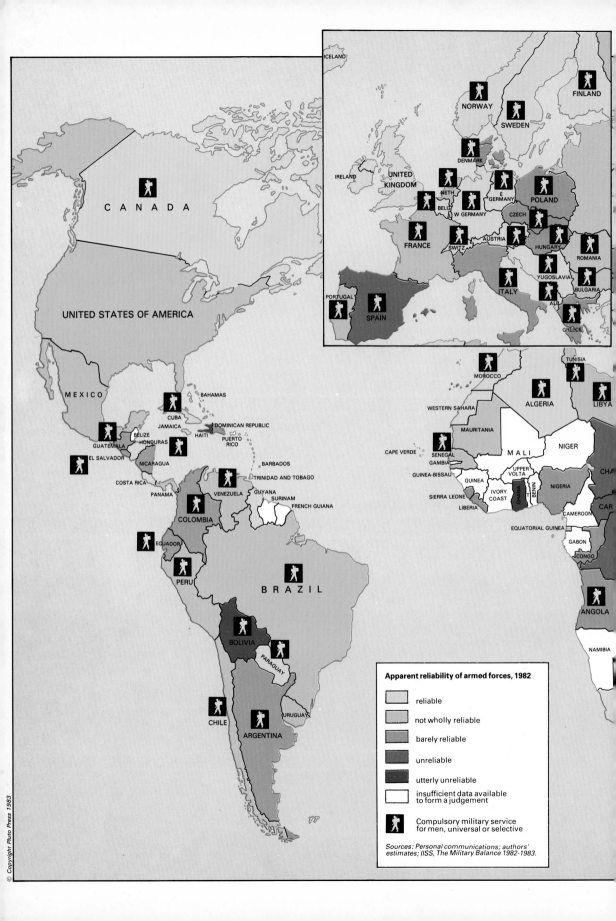

ICELAND
NORWAY
SWEDEN
FINLAND
DENMARK
IRELAND
UNITED KINGDOM
NETH
BELG
E GERMANY
W GERMANY
POLAND
CZECH
FRANCE
SWITZ
AUSTRIA
HUNGARY
ROMANIA
YUGOSLAVIA
BULGARIA
ITALY
ALB
PORTUGAL
SPAIN
GREECE

CANADA

UNITED STATES OF AMERICA

MEXICO

BAHAMAS
CUBA
JAMAICA
DOMINICAN REPUBLIC
HAITI
PUERTO RICO
GUATEMALA
BELIZE
HONDURAS
EL SALVADOR
NICARAGUA
COSTA RICA
PANAMA
BARBADOS
TRINIDAD AND TOBAGO
VENEZUELA
GUYANA
SURINAM
FRENCH GUIANA
COLOMBIA
ECUADOR
PERU
BRAZIL
BOLIVIA
PARAGUAY
CHILE
URUGUAY
ARGENTINA

TUNISIA
MOROCCO
ALGERIA
LIBYA
WESTERN SAHARA
MAURITANIA
MALI
NIGER
CAPE VERDE
SENEGAL
GAMBIA
GUINEA-BISSAU
GUINEA
IVORY COAST
UPPER VOLTA
GHANA
BENIN
NIGERIA
CHA
SIERRA LEONE
LIBERIA
CAR
CAMEROON
EQUATORIAL GUINEA
GABON
CONGO
ANGOLA
NAMIBIA

Apparent reliability of armed forces, 1982

reliable

not wholly reliable

barely reliable

unreliable

utterly unreliable

insufficient data available
to form a judgement

Compulsory military service
for men, universal or selective

*Sources: Personal communications; authors'
estimates; IISS, The Military Balance 1982-1983.*

© Copyright Pluto Press 1983

Armed forces are not always the dependable servants of the state. Incomplete loyalty and low morale make most forces less than reliable.

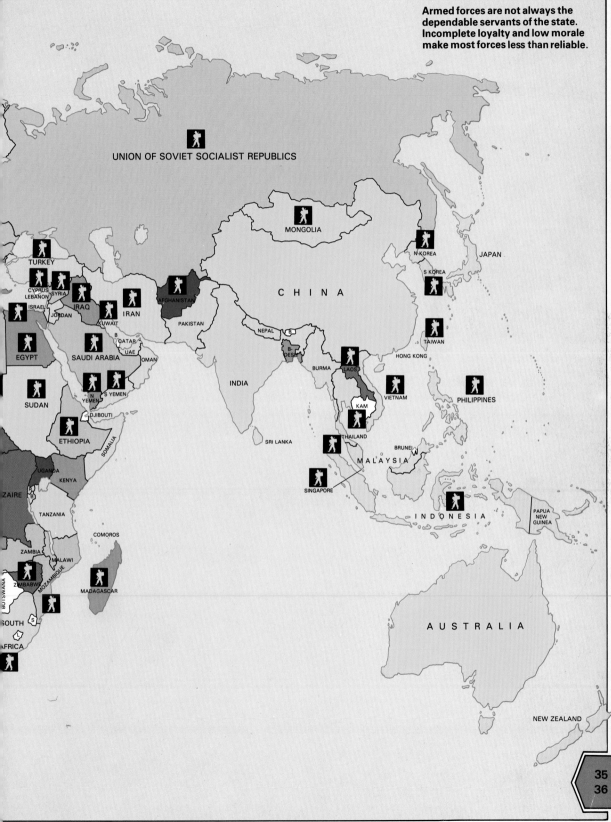

UNION OF SOVIET SOCIALIST REPUBLICS

MONGOLIA

N-KOREA

JAPAN

S KOREA

C H I N A

TURKEY

CYPRUS
LEBANON SYRIA
ISRAEL
JORDAN IRAQ
KUWAIT
AFGHANISTAN
PAKISTAN
IRAN

TAIWAN

NEPAL
B
B-DESH
BURMA
HONG KONG

EGYPT
B QATAR
UAE
OMAN
SAUDI ARABIA

LAOS

VIETNAM

PHILIPPINES

SUDAN
N YEMEN
S YEMEN
DJIBOUTI
SOMALIA

INDIA

SRI LANKA

KAM

THAILAND

BRUNEI

ETHIOPIA

UGANDA
KENYA

M A L A Y S I A

SINGAPORE

ZAIRE
B
B
TANZANIA

COMOROS

I N D O N E S I A

PAPUA
NEW
GUINEA

ZAMBIA
MALAWI
MOZAMBIQUE
ZIMBABWE
MADAGASCAR

A U S T R A L I A

BOTSWANA
SOUTH
AFRICA
S

NEW ZEALAND

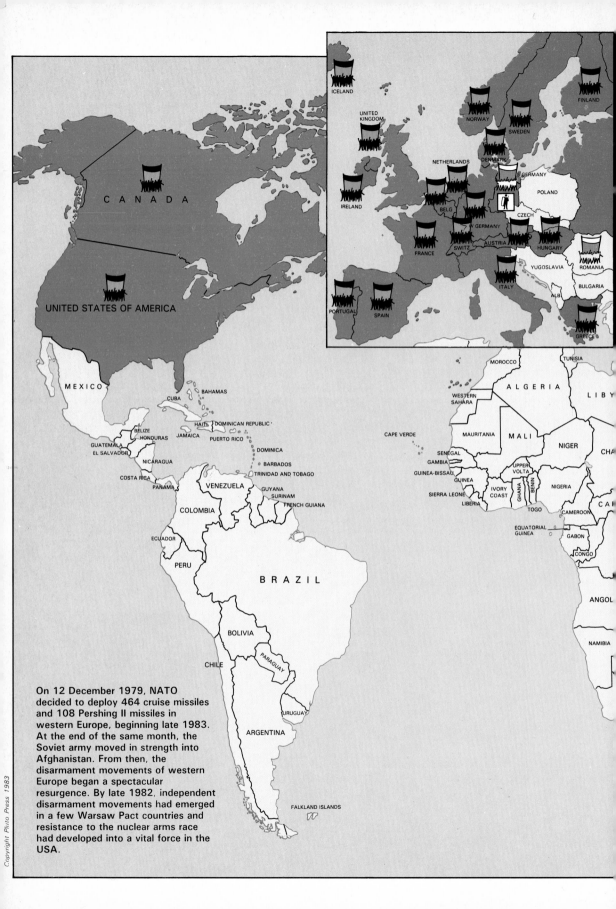

On 12 December 1979, NATO
decided to deploy 464 cruise missiles
and 108 Pershing II missiles in
western Europe, beginning late 1983.
At the end of the same month, the
Soviet army moved in strength into
Afghanistan. From then, the
disarmament movements of western
Europe began a spectacular
resurgence. By late 1982, independent
disarmament movements had emerged
in a few Warsaw Pact countries and
resistance to the nuclear arms race
had developed into a vital force in the
USA.

40. A New Order ?

Approximately two and a half million people took part in disarmament demonstrations in Europe in the last three months of 1981.

UNION OF SOVIET SOCIALIST REPUBLICS

MONGOLIA

N KOREA

S KOREA

JAPAN

CHINA

TURKEY

CYPRUS
LEBANON
SYRIA
ISRAEL
JORDAN
IRAQ
KUWAIT

AFGHANISTAN

IRAN

PAKISTAN

NEPAL
BHUTAN

B-
DESH

TAIWAN

EGYPT

QATAR
UAE
OMAN

SAUDI ARABIA

INDIA

BURMA

HONG
KONG

LAOS

THAILAND

KAM

VIETNAM

PHILIPPINES

SUDAN

N
YEMEN
S YEMEN

DJIBOUTI

ETHIOPIA

SOMALIA

SRI LANKA

IRE

UGANDA
B

KENYA

TANZANIA

COMOROS

BRUNEI

MALAYSIA

SINGAPORE

INDONESIA

PAPUA NEW GUINEA

AMBIA
MALAWI

ZIMBABWE
MOZAMBIQUE

MADAGASCAR

TH
RICA
S

Disarmament movements
December 1979 — October 1982

countries with independent movements or committees

others

Our definition of 'independent' movements and committees excludes groups which owe their policy and often their finances to one or other bloc or superpower.
Affiliates of the World Peace Council are thus excluded, as are the various committees in western European countries which propagandise for NATO.

major independent disarmament rallies and demonstrations

major state-sponsored disarmament rallies and demonstrations

official harrassment or suppression of independent disarmament movements, 1982

Sources: END; personal communications; press reports.

AUSTRALIA

NEW ZEALAND

	area 000 km²	population mid-1980 millions	political regime mid-1982	military expenditure 1981 US $m	military personnel mid-1982 000s	reliability of military 1982	years at war 1945-82	foreign wars 1945-82
Afghanistan	647	15.9	military	85	46.0	utterly unreliable	10	1
Albania	29	2.7	one-party	127	43.1	reliable	4	1
Algeria	2382	18.9	one-party	675	168.0	reliable	15	—
Angola	1247	7.1	one-party	n.a.	37.5	barely reliable	22	—
Argentina	2767	27.7	military	2241	180.5	barely reliable	9	—
Australia	7687	14.5	multi-party parliamentary	3508	73.2	reliable	7	2
Austria	84	7.5	multi-party parliamentary	847	49.4	reliable	—	—
Bahrain	0.6	0.4	despotic (not military)	115	2.6	n.a.	—	—
Bangladesh	144	90.2	restricted parliamentary	140	77.0	barely reliable	8	—
Barbados	0.4	0.2	multi-party parliamentary	n.a.	0.2	n.a.	—	—
Belgium	30	9.8	multi-party parliamentary	3690	93.5	reliable	6	2
Benin	113	3.5	military	23	3.2	n.a.	2	—
Bhutan	47	1.3	despotic (not military)	n.a.	n.a.	n.a.	—	—
Bolivia	1099	5.6	military	84	26.6	utterly unreliable	23	—
Botswana	600	0.8	multi-party parliamentary	29	3.0	n.a.	1	—
Brazil	8512	118.7	military	1234	272.9	probably reliable	3	—
Bulgaria	111	9.0	one-party	964	148.0	probably reliable	5	2
Burma	677	33.3	one-party	225	179.0	reliable	38	—
Burundi	28	4.1	military	23	5.2	reliable	3	—
Cameroon	475	8.4	one-party	82	7.3	n.a.	8	—
Canada	9976	23.9	multi-party parliamentary	4227	82.9	reliable	4	1
Central African Republic	623	2.3	multi-party parliamentary	12	2.3	unreliable	1	—
Chad	1284	4.5	military	62	3.2	unreliable	18	—
Chile	757	11.1	military	225	97.0	probably reliable	6	—
China	9597	976.7	one-party	37,200	4000.0	reliable	26	1
Colombia	1139	26.7	restricted parliamentary	229	67.8	barely reliable	29	1
Congo	342	1.5	military	68	8.7	barely reliable	4	—
Costa Rica	51	2.2	multi-party parliamentary	19	7.0	reliable	8	—
Cuba	115	9.9	one-party	1065	127.5	reliable	17	3
Cyprus	9	0.6	restricted parliamentary	19	10.0	n.a.	9	—
Czechoslovakia	128	15.3	one-party	2900	196.5	barely reliable	4	—
Denmark	43	5.1	multi-party parliamentary	1546	31.2	barely reliable	—	—
Djibouti	22	0.4	—	3	2.7	n.a.	4	—
Dominica	0.4	0.1	multi-party parliamentary	n.a.	n.a.	n.a.	2	—
Dominican Republic	49	5.4	multi-party parliamentary	92	24.5	barely reliable	12	—
Ecuador	283	8.4	multi-party parliamentary	92	38.8	barely reliable	3	—
Egypt	1001	39.8	restricted parliamentary	1650	452.0	barely reliable	19	5
Sources			see Map 35	see Map 23	see Map 26	see Map 39	see Maps 1-4	see Maps 1-

The International Military Order

at war in 1982	nuclear weapon status 1982	cold war orientation mid-1982	switched sides (S) or unreliable ally (U)	host to military bases of: mid-1982	countries hosting military bases number	world arms exports 1977-80 percentages	world arms imports 1977-80 percentages	
yes		core-East	S/U	USSR	–	–	0.5	Afghanistan
no		non-aligned	S	–	–	–	n.a.	Albania
no		non-aligned	S	–	–	–	1.5	Algeria
yes		pro-East	U	USSR/Cuba	–	–	0.7	Angola
yes	serious risk	pro-West	–	–	–	0.061	1.1	Argentina
no		core-West	–	USA/UK	2	0.63	0.9	Australia
no	capable	pro-West	–	–	–	0.075	0.1	Austria
no		pro-West	U	USA	–	–	0.02	Bahrain
no		non-aligned	S	–	–	–	0.07	Bangladesh
no		pro-West	–	–	–	–	n.a.	Barbados
no	capable	core-West	–	USA/W. Ger	–	0.0017	1.7	Belgium
no		pro-West	–	–	–	–	0.03	Benin
no		pro-West	–	India	–	–	n.a.	Bhutan
no		pro-West	–	–	–	–	0.1	Bolivia
no		pro-West	–	–	–	–	0.01	Botswana
no	serious risk	pro-West	–	USA	–	0.73	1.1	Brazil
no	capable	core-East	–	USSR	–	–	0.3	Bulgaria
yes		non-aligned	–	–	–	–	0.4	Burma
no		pro-West	U	–	–	–	n.a.	Burundi
no		pro-West	–	–	–	–	0.1	Cameroon
no	capable	core-West	–	USA/UK	2	0.31	0.8	Canada
no		pro-West	–	France	–	–	0.0006	Central African Republic
yes		pro-West	U	France/Libya	–	–	0.1	Chad
yes		pro-West	–	–	–	0.00017	0.8	Chile
no	known	non-aligned	S	–	–	0.58	0.1	China
yes		pro-West	–	–	–	–	0.08	Colombia
no		pro-East	S/U	–	–	–	0.006	Congo
no		pro-West	–	–	–	–	0.009	Costa Rica
yes	capable	core-East	S	USSR/USA	2	0.026	0.4	Cuba
no		pro-West	–	UK/Greece/Turkey	–	–	n.a.	Cyprus
no	capable	core-East	–	USSR	–	0.19	1.4	Czechoslovakia
no	capable	core-West	–	USA/W. Ger	–	–	0.7	Denmark
yes		pro-West	–	France/USA	–	–	0.009	Djibouti
no		pro-West	–	–	–	–	n.a.	Dominica
no		pro-West	–	–	–	–	0.004	Dominican Republic
yes		pro-West	–	–	–	–	0.5	Ecuador
no	capable	pro-West	S	USA	–	0.13	1.0	Egypt

| see Maps 1-4 | see Map 10 | see Map 16 | see Map 16 | see Map 17 | see Map 17 | see Map 30 | see Map 31 | |

	area 000 km²	population mid-1980 millions	political regime mid-1982	military expenditure 1981 US $m	military personnel mid-1982 000s	reliability of military 1982	years at war 1945-82	foreign wars 1945-82
El Salvador	21	4.5	restricted parliamentary	86	16.0	barely reliable	13	–
Equatorial Guinea	28	0.4	military	5	1.6	probably reliable	2	–
Ethiopia	1222	31.5	military	485	250.5	probably reliable	15	1
Fiji	18	0.6	multi-party parliamentary	4	2.1	reliable	–	–
Finland	337	4.9	multi-party parliamentary	632	36.9	reliable	–	–
France	547	53.5	multi-party parliamentary	23,633	492.9	probably reliable	38	21
Gabon	268	0.6	one-party	72	2.2	n.a.	1	–
Gambia	11	0.6	multi-party parliamentary	n.a.	n.a.	n.a.	1	–
Germany, East	108	16.9	one-party	4394	166.0	reliable	1	1
Germany, West	249	60.9	multi-party parliamentary	25,509	495.0	reliable	–	–
Ghana	238	11.7	military	110	14.6	utterly unreliable	1	–
Greece	132	9.3	multi-party parliamentary	2184	206.5	barely reliable	10	1
Grenada	0.8	0.1	one-party	n.a.	n.a.	n.a.	–	–
Guatemala	109	7.0	military	95	18.6	barely reliable	4	–
Guinea	246	5.4	one-party	44	9.9	n.a.	1	–
Guinea-Bissau	36	0.8	military	n.a.	6.3	n.a.	12	–
Guyana	215	0.8	restricted parliamentary	27	7.0	reliable	6	–
Haiti	28	5.0	despotic (not military)	22	7.5	utterly unreliable	4	–
Honduras	112	3.7	military	38	11.7	reliable	9	2
Hungary	93	10.8	one-party	810	106.0	barely reliable	3	1
Iceland	103	0.2	multi-party parliamentary	n.a.	n.a.	reliable	–	–
India	3288	673.2	multi-party parliamentary	3991	1104.0	reliable	24	4
Indonesia	1904	146.2	military	1426	2690.0	reliable	30	1
Iran	1648	38.1	despotic (not military)	5092	2350.0	reliable	13	2
Iraq	435	13.1	one-party	3759	342.3	barely reliable	11	1
Ireland	70	3.3	multi-party parliamentary	246	16.4	reliable	–	1
Israel	21	3.9	restricted parliamentary	2750	174.0	reliable	14	5
Italy	301	56.9	multi-party parliamentary	8184	370.0	barely reliable	7	–
Ivory Coast	322	8.6	one-party	111	5.1	n.a.	4	–
Jamaica	11	2.2	multi-party parliamentary	29	1.7	reliable	–	–
Japan	372	116.6	multi-party parliamentary	9461	245.0	reliable	–	–
Jordan	98	3.2	despotic (not military)	420	72.8	reliable	10	3
Kampuchea	181	5.1	one-party	n.a.	20.0	n.a.	29	1
Kenya	583	15.9	one-party	183	16.7	barely reliable	9	–
Korea, North	121	17.9	one-party	3424	784.0	reliable	8	–
Korea, South	98	38.5	restricted parliamentary	3519	601.6	reliable	12	1
Kuwait	18	1.4	despotic (not military)	2031	12.4	reliable	3	–

at war in 1982	nuclear weapon status 1982	cold war orientation mid-1982	switched sides (S) or unreliable ally (U)	host to military bases of: mid-1982	countries hosting military bases number	world arms exports 1977-80 percentages	world arms imports 1977-80 percentages	
yes		pro-West	U	—	—	—	0.03	El Salvador
no		pro-West	S	—	—	—	0.00007	Equatorial Guinea
yes		pro-East	S/U	USSR/Cuba/ S. Yemen	—	—	1.9	Ethiopia
no		pro-West	—	—	—	—	n.a.	Fiji
no	capable	non-aligned	—	—	—	0.19	0.8	Finland
yes	known	core-West	—	—	17	10.8	0.06	France
no		pro-West	—	France	—	—	0.2	Gabon
no		pro-West	—	—	—	—	n.a.	Gambia
no	capable	core-East	—	USSR	—	—	1.1	Germany, East
no	capable	core-West	—	USA/UK/F/ B/Can/N	6	3.0	1.3	Germany, West
no		pro-West	S/U	—	—	—	0.2	Ghana
no		core-West	—	USA	1	—	3.3	Greece
no		non-aligned	S	—	—	—	n.a.	Grenada
yes		pro-West	U	USA	—	—	0.03	Guatemala
no		non-aligned	S	—	—	—	0.02	Guinea
no		non-aligned	—	—	—	—	0.03	Guinea-Bissau
no		pro-West	U	—	—	—	n.a.	Guyana
no		pro-West	—	—	—	—	n.a.	Haiti
yes		pro-West	U	—	—	—	0.09	Honduras
no	capable	core-East	—	USSR	—	0.0087	0.4	Hungary
no		core-West	—	USA	—	0.0017	n.a.	Iceland
no	known	non-aligned	—	—	—	0.021	3.4	India
yes		pro-West	S	—	1	0.029	0.9	Indonesia
yes	serious risk	non-aligned	S/U	—	—	—	6.0	Iran
yes	serious risk	non-aligned	S/U	—	—	0.017	3.8	Iraq
no		pro-West	—	—	—	0.077	0.03	Ireland
yes	suspected	pro-West	—	—	1	0.64	3.1	Israel
no	capable	core-West	—	UK/USA/ W. Ger	—	4.0	3.8	Italy
no		pro-West	—	France	—	—	0.2	Ivory Coast
no		pro-West	—	—	—	—	0.001	Jamaica
no	capable	core-West	—	USA	—	0.061	2.6	Japan
no		pro-West	U	—	—	—	4.5	Jordan
yes		pro-East	S	Vietnam	—	—	0.1	Kampuchea
yes		pro-West	—	—	—	—	0.3	Kenya
no		pro-East	—	—	—	0.007	0.1	Korea, North
no	serious risk	core-West	—	USA	—	0.07	3.5	Korea, South
no		pro-West	—	—	—	—	1.2	Kuwait

see Maps 1-4   see Map 10   see Map 16   see Map 16   see Map 17   see Map 17   see Map 30   see Map 31

	area	population	political regime	military expenditure	military personnel	reliability of military	years at war	foreign wars
	000 km²	mid-1980 millions	mid-1982	1981 US $m	mid-1982 000s	1982	1945-82	1945-8
Laos	237	3.4	one-party	21	48.7	unreliable	30	–
Lebanon	10	2.7	multi-party parliamentary	325	23.8	barely reliable	12	2
Lesotho	30	1.3	despotic (not military)	n.a.	n.a.	n.a.	–	–
Liberia	111	1.9	military	16	5.4	barely reliable	–	–
Libya	1760	3.0	despotic (not military)	3670	65.0	probably reliable	10	1
Luxembourg	3	0.4	multi-party parliamentary	51	0.7	reliable	4	1
Madagascar	587	8.7	one-party	71	20.9	barely reliable	4	–
Malawi	118	6.0	despotic (not military)	22	4.7	probably reliable	8	–
Malaysia	330	13.4	multi-party parliamentary	1639	99.1	reliable	22	–
Mali	1240	6.9	military	46	5.0	n.a.	2	–
Malta	0.3	0.3	multi-party parliamentary	11	0.8	n.a.	–	–
Mauritania	1031	1.6	military	82	8.5	probably reliable	11	1
Mauritius	2	1.0	multi-party parliamentary	2	n.a.	n.a.	–	–
Mexico	1972	67.5	restricted parliamentary	782	119.5	probably reliable	1	–
Mongolia	1565	1.7	one-party	238	34.6	reliable	–	–
Morocco	446	20.2	despotic (not military)	1005	141.0	reliable	19	3
Mozambique	783	10.5	one-party	111	21.6	probably reliable	14	–
Nepal	141	14.3	despotic (not military)	28	25.0	reliable	2	–
Netherlands	41	14.1	multi-party parliamentary	4931	104.0	probably reliable	8	2
New Zealand	269	3.3	multi-party parliamentary	393	12.9	reliable	4	1
Nicaragua	130	2.7	restricted parliamentary	34	21.5	barely reliable	33	3
Niger	1267	5.3	military	16	2.2	n.a.	–	–
Nigeria	924	84.8	restricted parliamentary	2037	138.0	barely reliable	4	–
Norway	324	4.1	multi-party parliamentary	1484	421.0	reliable	–	–
Oman	212	0.9	despotic (not military)	1444	18.0	reliable	10	–
Pakistan	804	82.2	military	1307	478.6	reliable	13	3
Panama	76	1.8	restricted parliamentary	22	9.0	probably reliable	1	–
Papua New Guinea	462	3.0	multi-party parliamentary	n.a.	3.8	reliable	1	1
Paraguay	407	3.1	military	40	16.0	reliable	5	–
Peru	1285	17.6	multi-party parliamentary	480	135.5	probably reliable	8	–
Philippines	300	47.9	restricted parliamentary	688	112.8	reliable	26	1
Poland	313	35.8	military	2467	317.0	barely reliable	5	2
Portugal	92	9.8	multi-party parliamentary	779	66.4	probably reliable	15	4
Qatar	11	0.2	despotic (not military)	893	6.0	n.a.	–	–
Romania	238	22.3	one-party	1285	181.0	probably reliable	1	–
Rwanda	26	5.1	military	18	5.2	reliable	5	

at war in 1982	nuclear weapon status 1982	cold war orientation mid-1982	switched sides (S) or unreliable ally (U)	host to military bases of: mid-1982	countries hosting military bases number	world arms exports 1977-80 percentages	world arms imports 1977-80 percentages	
no		pro-East	S	Vietnam	–	–	0.08	Laos
yes		pro-West	–	Israel/Syria	–	–	0.07	Lebanon
no		pro-West	–	–	–	–	0.00007	Lesotho
no		pro-West	–	USA	–	–	0.02	Liberia
yes	serious risk	pro-East	S	–	1	0.17	3.7	Libya
no		core-West	–	USA	–	–	n.a.	Luxembourg
no		pro-West	U	France	–	–	0.09	Madagascar
no		pro-West	–	–	–	–	0.02	Malawi
no		pro-West	–	–	1	–	0.6	Malaysia
no		pro-West	S	–	–	–	n.a.	Mali
no		pro-West	–	UK	–	–	0.008	Malta
no		pro-West	–	–	–	–	0.06	Mauritania
no		pro-West	–	France	–	–	0.03	Mauritius
no	capable	pro-West	–	–	–	–	0.1	Mexico
no		core-East	–	USSR	–	–	n.a.	Mongolia
yes		pro-West	–	Spain	1	0.0017	2.0	Morocco
yes		pro-East	–	–	–	–	0.3	Mozambique
no		pro-West	–	–	–	–	n.a.	Nepal
no	capable	core-West	–	USA/W. Ger	3	0.93	1.8	Netherlands
no		core-West	–	USA	1	0.0017	0.04	New Zealand
yes		non-aligned	S/U	–	–	–	0.02	Nicaragua
no		pro-West	–	–	–	–	0.03	Niger
no		pro-West	–	–	–	–	0.3	Nigeria
no	capable	core-West	–	USA/UK	–	1.3	0.1	Norway
yes		pro-West	U	USA/UK	–	–	0.3	Oman
no	serious risk	pro-West	U	–	–	–	0.9	Pakistan
no		pro-West	–	USA	–	–	0.02	Panama
no		pro-West	–	–	–	–	0.004	Papua New Guinea
no		pro-West	–	–	–	–	0.02	Paraguay
yes		pro-West	–	–	–	–	1.7	Peru
yes	capable	pro-West	U	USA	1	–	0.5	Philippines
yes	capable	core-East	U	USSR	–	0.11	1.6	Poland
no	capable	core-West	–	USA/Can/UK W. Ger/N	1	0.033	0.1	Portugal
no		pro-West	–	–	–	–	0.1	Qatar
no	capable	core-East	U	–	–	0.0035	0.6	Romania
no		pro-West	U	–	–	–	0.001	Rwanda

ee Maps 1-4   see Map 10   see Map 16   see Map 16   see Map 17   see Map 17   see Map 30   see Map 31

	area 000 km²	population mid-1980 millions	political regime mid-1982	military expenditure 1981 US $m	military personnel mid-1982 000s	reliability of military 1982	years at war 1945-82	foreign wars 1945-8.
Saudi Arabia	2150	9.0	despotic (not military)	22,458	52.2	probably reliable	2	–
Seychelles	0.3	0.06	one-party	n.a.	1.0	n.a.	1	–
Sierra Leone	72	3.5	restricted parliamentary	19	3.2	barely reliable	–	–
Singapore	0.6	2.4	one-party	556	42.0	reliable	–	–
Somalia	638	3.9	military	150	62.6	reliable	3	1
South Africa	1221	29.3	restricted parliamentary	2254	81.4	reliable	13	2
Spain	505	37.4	multi-party parliamentary	3682	347.0	unreliable	3	–
Sri Lanka	66	14.8	multi-party parliamentary	35	16.4	reliable	2	–
Sudan	2506	18.4	one-party	470	580.0	reliable	19	–
Surinam	163	0.4	military	n.a.	0.8	n.a.	1	–
Swaziland	17	0.6	despotic (not military)	n.a.	5.0	n.a.	–	–
Sweden	450	8.3	multi-party parliamentary	3175	64.5	reliable	–	–
Switzerland	41	6.5	multi-party parliamentary	2000	20.0	reliable	–	–
Syria	185	9.0	one-party	2166	222.5	probably reliable	15	5
Taiwan	36	17.6	one-party	2456	464.0	reliable	4	–
Tanzania	945	18.1	one-party	285	40.4	reliable	6	1
Thailand	514	46.5	military	1036	233.1	reliable	14	2
Togo	57	2.5	military	22	3.6	n.a.	–	–
Trinidad and Tobago	5	1.2	multi-party parliamentary	12	20.0	reliable	–	–
Tunisia	164	6.4	one-party	214	28.6	probably reliable	9	–
Turkey	781	45.4	military	3442	569.0	reliable	12	3
Uganda	236	13.2	restricted parliamentary	852	5.0	utterly unreliable	9	1
United Arab Emirates	84	0.9	despotic (not military)	1423	48.5	reliable	1	–
United Kingdom	244	55.9	multi-party parliamentary	19,901	327.6	reliable	37	29
Upper Volta	274	5.7	military	41	3.8	n.a.	2	–
Uruguay	176	2.9	military	150	29.7	probably reliable	6	–
USA	9363	227.3	multi-party parliamentary	134,390	2116.8	probably reliable	25	13
USSR	22,402	266.7	one-party	118,800	3705.0	probably reliable	19	6
Venezuela	912	14.9	multi-party parliamentary	527	40.8	probably reliable	13	1
Vietnam	330	54.2	one-party	n.a.	1029.0	reliable	34	3
Western Samoa	3	0.2	multi-party parliamentary	n.a.	n.a.	n.a.	–	–
Yemen, North	195	5.8	military	320	32.1	barely reliable	16	–
Yemen, South	333	1.9	one-party	115	26.0	reliable	20	1
Yugoslavia	256	22.3	one-party	2936	250.5	reliable	5	1
Zaire	2345	28.3	despotic (not military)	164	26.0	unreliable	10	–
Zambia	753	5.8	one-party	290	14.3	probably reliable	5	–
Zimbabwe	391	7.4	multi-party parliamentary	440	63.0	unreliable	17	–

at war in 1982	nuclear weapon status 1982	cold war orientation mid-1982	switched sides (S) or unreliable ally (U)	host to military bases of: mid-1982	countries hosting military bases number	world arms exports 1977-80 percentages	world arms imports 1977-80 percentages	
no		pro-West	–	USA	–	0.054	5.5	Saudi Arabia
yes		pro-West	–	–	–	–	0.0008	Seychelles
no		pro-West	–	–	–	–	0.001	Sierra Leone
no		pro-West	–	Australia/NZ/Malaysia	–	0.03	0.4	Singapore
yes		pro-West	S/U	USA	–	–	0.2	Somalia
yes	suspected	pro-West	–	–	1	0.2	1.7	South Africa
yes	capable	core-West	–	USA	1	0.11	1.9	Spain
no		non-aligned	–	–	–	–	0.02	Sri Lanka
no		pro-West	S	–	–	0.016	0.2	Sudan
no		pro-West	U	–	–	–	0.03	Surinam
no		pro-West	–	–	–	–	0.01	Swaziland
no	capable	non-aligned	–	–	–	0.48	1.4	Sweden
no	capable	non-aligned	–	–	–	0.42	0.6	Switzerland
yes		pro-East	S/U	USSR	1	–	4.0	Syria
no	serious risk	pro-West	U	USA	1	0.0035	1.3	Taiwan
no		non-aligned	–	–	–	–	0.1	Tanzania
yes		pro-West	U	USA	–	0.017	0.7	Thailand
no		pro-West	U	–	–	–	0.07	Togo
no		pro-West	–	–	–	–	0.03	Trinidad and Tobago
no		pro-West	–	–	–	–	0.2	Tunisia
no	capable	core-West	U	USA	1	–	1.8	Turkey
yes		pro-West	U	–	–	–	0.001	Uganda
no		pro-West	–	–	–	–	0.4	United Arab Emirates
yes	known	core-West	–	USA	17	3.7	1.0	United Kingdom
no		pro-West	–	–	–	–	0.006	Upper Volta
no		pro-West	–	–	–	–	0.02	Uruguay
yes	known	core-West	–	–	46	43.3	0.2	United States
yes	known	core-East	–	–	13	27.4	0.3	USSR
no		pro-West	–	–	–	–	0.4	Venezuela
yes		core-East	S	USSR	3	–	2.1	Vietnam
no		pro-West	–	–	–	–	–	Western Samoa
no		pro-West	S/U	–	–	–	0.5	Yemen, North
no		pro-East	S/U	USSR	1	–	1.7	Yemen, South
yes	capable	non-aligned	S	–	–	0.085	0.3	Yugoslavia
no		pro-West	–	–	–	–	0.1	Zaire
no		pro-West	–	–	–	–	0.06	Zambia
yes		pro-West	–	–	–	–	0.2	Zimbabwe

see Maps 1-4   see Map 10   see Map 16   see Map 16   see Map 17   see Map 17   see Map 30   see Map 31

Notes to the Maps

1. A World at War
2. War since 1945: Americas
3. War since 1945: Europe, Middle East, Africa
4. War since 1945: Asia, Pacific

All wars involve human suffering, and to that extent they are all the same. But all wars are fought for specific purposes, and to that extent they are different. In these maps we have identified wars and war zones, then organised wars into certain categories, fully conscious that by doing so we have imposed fixed definitions onto a reality which is complex and constantly changing. The cold war has been and is being actively fought by proxy in many places, usually as an adjunct of another type of war: Korea in the early 1950s or Southern Africa and Central America today. Some states' border wars are others' general wars: for example, the Indo-Pakistan conflict of 1971 or the Sino-Indian conflict of 1962. Local civil wars often merge with interstate wars, as in Ethiopia's war in the Ogaden region; or develop, often imperceptibly, into general wars, as with every victorious guerilla campaign from China in the late forties to Nicaragua thirty years later.

Even the definition of war itself is arbitrary. For example, when does fighting become war? As wars of lesser intensity, we include the 'dirty war' in Argentina in the late 1970s, the sporadic fighting between the ANC guerillas and the South African government, and many similar cases. But we do not include, for example, the armed confrontations between the Red Brigades and the state in Italy in the 1970s, or the Black Panthers and the state in the USA in the 1960s.

We do not show UN peacekeeping missions: only actual warfighting features in these maps. Logistical support, training, the supply and servicing of weapons, shows of force short of hostilities and employment of mercenaries have been excluded on practical grounds. In part they are taken up elsewhere.

There is a measure of political judgement in these maps, notably in the treatment of claims to victory and the assessment of the historic context for a hostile act — whether it forms part of a run of similar events, or a discrete event, or part of a larger event. For example, we have ignored Iraq's repeated claims of victory over the Kurds; we have ignored border wars that preceded or followed general wars between neighbours. We have treated some annexations, such as Libya's of the Aozou strip in Chad (1973), as border wars; and others, such as Israel's of the West Bank or Golan Heights, not.

There is also a measure of judgement in assigning dates. It has always been difficult to know when a war has started or ended. It is especially difficult now that formal declarations of hostility are exceptions to the rule of war-by-stealth or by surprise. The difficulties are compounded when the contestants have different assessments of the war they are fighting: the USA government saw in Vietnam a salient of cold war, whereas the Vietnamese saw civil conflict with outside interference; for the Russians, Afghanistan is an arena for civil war, whereas many Afghans feel they are fighting a foreign occupying power. We have tried to take a broad historic view of the conflicts and to differentiate as many strands as our knowledge and space allow. Anti-colonial and similar wars have been classified as civil wars with foreign presence.

We have not allowed our conception of right or wrong, or our judgement of long-term viability, to sway our designation of victor. In all cases of active civil war, victory has been assigned to the government recognised internationally in mid-1982. Only where power has been transferred without the agreement of the pre-war government and there has been no continuity of policy has 'change in regime' been indicated. We have therefore excluded Guatemala (1982) from this designation, and all cases where a government, pressed by insurgents, has handed over power to the military.

6. Caught in the Crossfire
Some civil wars are fought only abroad, like the Armenian-Turkish or Croatian-Yugoslav wars. Some are fought abroad as well as in the disputed home territory,

like the Palestine-Israel war. Some, like the Basque-Spanish war, spill into neighbouring foreign territory – France in this case – and some are seldom felt outside the country of war. Other people's civil wars, fought in accordance with a logic and timetable unfamiliar in the host country, are particularly savage in striking at innocent victims. This map records some of the occasions, over a three-year period, on which third parties were caught up in conflicts not of their choosing.

The map includes incidents in a foreign country not party to the original dispute; incidents in what is technically home territory abroad; and incidents in what is technically foreign territory in the country of civil war, such as an embassy or consular building. Of course the information is neither comprehensive nor particularly reliable: many incidents are recorded in the sources without background or explanation and the recording itself is narrowly NATO-centric.

The map does not include the large number of incidents on territory regarded as foreign by only one party in the dispute, such as mainland Britain (foreign for the Irish republicans), France (for Corsican separatists), Spain (for Basque separatists), Israel (for Palestinians). Nor does it include hot pursuits or cross-border raids on sanctuaries by the armed forces, as in the case of South African incursions into neighbouring states, Afghani into northern Pakistan, Vietnamese into Thailand. The map also excludes hijackings, and attacks on foreigners or foreign property seen as parties to a domestic dispute: for example, attacks by right-wingers in France on Soviet diplomats as part of a general anti-communist crusade.

Some third-party attacks reflect civil wars that have been raging and are likely to go on raging for a long time: Armenians, for example, continue to exact reprisals for the Turkish genocidal attack of 1915; Palestinians are attempting to reverse their dispossession of 1947-48. Other attacks are historic flashes reflecting a fleeting conjunction, such as the campaign of assassinations ordered by the Libyan government against exiled oppositionists in the first half of 1980; or the rash of Colombian embassy occupations following the military coup in July of that year.

This map shows only a small sample of the numerous manoeuvres and exercises conducted each year. Many such exercises involve little or no movement of troops: they are 'command exercises', testing out the command, control and communications systems which direct and monitor the movement of people and hardware. On this map, however, all the manoeuvres involved the deployment of very large numbers, in some cases over considerable distances.

7. Practice Makes Perfect

Under the agreement signed at the Conference on Security and Cooperation in Europe in 1975, exercises in Europe involving more than 25,000 troops must be notified in advance. NATO states habitually provide notification of smaller exercises as well. The three years shown were not chosen for any special significance; they were average years.

The public does not have access to the war-games and planning scenarios, which are used in official studies about the possible course of nuclear war. Information which has come into the public domain has not included details about how either the USA or the USSR considers a nuclear war could be conducted.

8. Ground Zero

In the absence of detailed and comprehensive official scenarios, the study conducted by *Ambio*, the environmental journal of the Royal Swedish Academy of Sciences, is particularly impressive. It depicts one feasible set of assumptions about what targets might be attacked, and what the consequences would be. It extends to a global level the many official and unofficial studies which have been made of the effects of nuclear war in single countries. The special issue of *Ambio* which reported this study is packed with gruesome details. We have summarised some of the most salient in the text on the map.

The information on targets in United States plans is taken from Ball, 1981.

Like *Maps 12-15*, this map provides a snapshot of military hardware at a particular moment. Many of the figures are suspect, relying, for example, on published US intelligence estimates of Chinese or Soviet weaponry. However, at this level of destructive potential, precise figures are less important than orders of magnitude.

9. The Nuclear Stockpile

China test-fired a submarine-launched ballistic missile (SLBM) in October 1982 and apparently has submarines capable of launching such missiles. By the end of the year China had not deployed any operational SLBMs but it was, presumably, only a matter of time until it did.

The numbers of strategic warheads shown for the USA and USSR are based on commonly made assumptions: as to how many multiple, independently targeted warheads are carried on strategic missiles; and how many bombs are carried on each aircraft. Similar figures are not provided for China, France and the UK because they do not deploy such warheads.

Although we use the common shorthand of 'missiles', it is 'missile launchers' which are actually counted. There may be more missiles than launchers (just as there are more shells than guns): in NATO, for example, there are commonly six or seven short-range missiles for each launcher. Similarly, there are more nuclear bombs than aircraft, more nuclear shells than cannon, and so on. Details on actual numbers of bombs, shells and warheads are neither easily nor fully available.

Among the stranger weapons, nuclear depth bombs are for use against submarines; and atomic demolition munitions are nuclear explosives which are buried and then detonated by a timer or command mechanism.

There is some doubt as to whether East Germany would have access to nuclear weapons in war: Western intelligence does not appear to be unanimous on this issue. In this map, as in *Map 13: On the Ground*, we have assumed that the East German army is nuclear armed.

10. Insecurity in Numbers A nuclear weapon state is one which has detonated a nuclear explosion.

There is some confusion over Vietnam's status in the Nuclear Non-Proliferation Treaty. Hanoi claimed to have ratified the treaty before our cut-off date (30 June 1982) while the Foreign Office in Britain, one of the three depository states for the treaty, disclaimed knowledge of this. Albania, Colombia and Kuwait had signed but not ratified the treaty by then. They were therefore not parties to it.

11. Bugs and Poisons US estimates of Soviet stockpiles of lethal gas range from 30,000 to several hundred thousand tons, and a quasi-official US figure for its stockpiles is 42,000 tons. One Soviet estimate of the US stockpile puts it at 300,000 tons, and the same source (Tass news agency) has denied that the USSR has any lethal gas at all. Estimates of the size of the French stockpile are not available.

Since it is believed that only the USA, the USSR and France manufacture lethal poison gas, allegations that other states are using it imply that one of these three has transferred it to an alleged user. But hard evidence is not available, and we do not know for sure that other states do not themselves manufacture lethal gases.

Since the first world war, when 115,000 tons of poison gas were used on the western front, the use of gas and germ warfare has been alleged more frequently than it has been proven. State secrecy and sensitivity make proof and disproof equally hard to come by. There is also much confusion between lethal gases and other kinds, such as tear gas, on the part of those making the allegations. Some of the allegations recorded on this map may be mere figments of propaganda, though we have excluded several which seem blatantly propagandistic and for which no supporting evidence has been advanced.

13. On the Ground The main source for these three maps is *The Military Balance*, published annually
14. In the Air by the International Institute for Strategic Studies (IISS) in London. There is no
15. At Sea other publication which lists systematically the armed forces of as many states.

The IISS's own sources include press reports, official publications, annual questionnaires to military attachés of embassies in London (from which the response rate is about 30 per cent), and military intelligence. These sources cannot be relied upon for complete honesty or accuracy and their imperfections are passed on in *The Military Balance*. Consequently, even where precise figures are provided, these three maps should be read with some caution, and comparisons of armed forces need to allow very broad margins of error.

In any case, numbers alone are not enough for a proper comparison of military effectiveness. For that, one needs to know more about the quality and age of the equipment; about the training, morale and experience of the personnel; about the functions of the armed forces, their tasks and the quality of their leadership. For information on some of these things see *Map 35: Military Rule, Map 36: The Military* as *Police* and *Map 39: Achilles' Heel*.

In *Map 13: On the Ground*, information about troop strengths excludes marines because they are included in *Map 15: At Sea*. For total military strengths, see *Map 26: Under Arms*.

For efficiency in war, personal experience of actual fighting is worth far more than a theoretical understanding. This experience is found among non-commissioned, middle rank and senior officers in armies which have fought wars in the past decade. Small border skirmishes and minor police actions do not spread this kind of experience within an army. That is why we have chosen to limit our category to 'major combat experience'.

In *Map 14: In the Air*, we have listed 'Counter-insurgency' (COIN) aircraft as a separate category. In fact, almost all aircraft can operate against insurgents. But some aircraft are especially designed for that task. They are generally light aircraft, often powered by only a single piston-engine, relatively unsophisticated but quite heavily armed. They would be useless in air-to-air combat, and vulnerable to modern surface-to-air missiles. Against lightly armed guerillas, however, they are well suited and very cost effective. The COIN designation is given by the manufacturers and the states which deploy them.

Since all helicopters can be armed, and almost all of them can be used for some kind of transport, we have not distinguished between armed and unarmed helicopters. Armed helicopters can be used, depending on their armament, against ships, submarines, tanks and other land targets and also for COIN.

Map 15: At Sea. The largest surface warships by far are the USA's aircraft carriers. These can accommodate more than 90 fixed-wing combat aircraft as well as helicopters. Of the eight other states which have aircraft carriers, only France's carry more than 30 aircraft.

In 1981, only four states were using nuclear-powered submarines other than as launching platforms for strategic nuclear missiles. The USSR had 99, the USA 79, the UK 12 and China 2. A fifth state, France, which already uses them to carry strategic missiles, was constructing its first nuclear-powered submarine for general purpose use. Compared with diesel-electric submarines, nuclear-powered vessels have a much greater range and can remain submerged for much longer — long enough to circumnavigate the globe under water.

This map represents our personal assessment of the political allegiances of the world's states in terms of the cold war. Some of the judgements will doubtless be contested. We would make two points. First, the categories in the map are deliberately broad and catch the main direction of states' policies rather than their nuances. Second, the categories are not symmetrical. The West has greater wealth and economic pulling power as well as a longer history. Consequently the USSR's allies are less numerous and relatively less dependable. They owe their allegiance mainly to the fact of geography and narrow, often short-term, political expediency.

16. Camps and Followers

The Caribbean island of Grenada ranks as a non-aligned state following a switch away from Western alignment due to a change in state power.

It is only recently that researchers have begun to locate and identify the thousands of foreign military bases and installations throughout the world. The work carries no little personal risk. In Britain, Norway and Sweden there have been arrests and trials of individuals who, using information already publicly available and the evidence of their own eyes, have made deductions which those states found embarrassingly accurate. It is hard to believe that their painstaking work produces more information than is already known to other states through satellite photography, spies and electronic intelligence.

17. A Corner of a Foreign Field

There are three senses in which a military installation may be a foreign base. First, the base may be in the territory of another sovereign state (for example, US or Soviet bases in West or East Germany). Second, it may be in territory under the jurisdiction of a third party (for example, the US base in Diego Garcia, leased from the British). Third, it may be in territory under the jurisdiction of the state which operates it (for example, the French bases in Guadeloupe).

We have not included 'port visits' in the category of 'port facilities' which, like 'landing rights', implies regular usage or special arrangements. We have included only combat forces in the category of 'army forces'. As supply depots we have listed only those which are not part of the infrastructure of other bases. Although only a single symbol of each kind is shown in any state or territory, in many cases this covers many bases.

18. A Little Help from their Friends Military training is more than education in particular skills and techniques; it is also an education in attitudes. Trainees are expected to learn particular ways of thinking about the appropriate role for armed forces, about how they should be organised and how they should act. Trainees also learn a particular 'correct' view of the world, of current affairs and modern history, of the uses and limitations of power.

Naturally, what is thought to be 'correct' varies from one state to another. Thus, in providing training for other states' armed forces, especially their officers, states such as Britain, France, the USA and the USSR are also attempting to gain allies within those other forces; allies who may well rise to positions of major power and influence. Despite the importance of the topic (or, perhaps, because of it), training and advice for foreign armed forces is under-researched. The information in this map therefore falls far short of being complete.

19. The Soviet Garrison The title of this map bears a double meaning. The USSR garrisons several other states — Eastern Europe, Afghanistan, Mongolia. It can also be seen, despite its size, as a beleaguered garrison, more or less ringed by committed anti-Soviet states. The projection used for this map accentuates this aspect, but is incomplete: for reasons of space alone, Canada and the USA could not be included, although they are geographically close. The distinction is clearest in the case of China. For more than a decade, China has been a most virulent anti-Soviet state, castigating the West for taking a soft line during detente. Yet it is not part of the Western camp.

The classification of states, as committed anti-Soviet or uncommitted, differs from the one used for *Map 16: Camps and Followers*. In that map, we relied on our own judgements, while for this one we have attempted to replicate those judgements that might be made in Moscow.

20. The US Network No other state has such a widespread or technologically sophisticated information and communication system as the USA. However, not all its components are financed or operated by the USA directly. Its network has been pieced together in a variety of ways. Some installations are jointly staffed and financed. Others are jointly staffed but with no US financing, or jointly financed but with no US staff. Yet other installations involve neither US finances nor staff, but they remain US assets, functioning as links in its chain of information and communication.

The USA has invested much capital in its network and many of the installations are vast. The Jim Creek Naval Radio Station in Washington state, for example, is a is a Very Low Frequency transmitter for communications with nuclear-armed submarines: 'Strung among 12 towers on two mountains east of Arlington is an awesome web of 25 miles of inch-thick copper cable. Draped systematically across the clear-cut valley floor are another 300 miles of heavy wire.' (*The Seattle Times*, 31 January 1982.)

Electronic intelligence stations are primarily concerned with intercepting radio communications, but in some cases are also used for listening in to telephone conversations. The National Military Command Centres in the USA are both the primary and back-up decision-making centres for times of crisis. The Worldwide Military Command and Communication System (WMCCS) is a relatively new chain of satellite-linked major communications stations: the 15 WMCCS sites in the USA have been excluded from the map for reasons of space. We were unable to identify other major ground terminals for satellite communications in the USA.

Cuba is shown as being part of the US network because the USA operates an electronic intelligence station at its Guantanamo base on the island. Other countries, France for example, are shown as part of the network, although no individual facilities are identified. These countries host only small installations in the Defense Communications System. There are so many of these that it was not feasible to include them in the map. Indeed, the size and spread of the US network is such that comprehensiveness has had to be sacrificed to comprehensibility. Not included on the map is Brazil, which hosts installations in the Defense Communications System, and:

	space satellite tracking station	electronic spying	nuclear armed submarines station	other
American Samoa	⌖			
Ascension Island	⌖	UK		
Azores				
Hawaii			⚓	O
Johnston Atoll	⌖		⚓	O
Liberia			⚓	
Micronesia				
Namibia		S. Africa		
New Zealand	⌖			
Réunion			France	
St Helena		UK		

There are two reasons for exercising force without war – to order the relations between equals, particularly the superpowers, and to police the rest. Many incidents are obscure. Often all we know about them with certainty is the location. The purpose, the perpetrator or even the intended victim may be unknown and of necessity imputed. We have concluded, for example, that unidentified submarines discovered off the coasts of Argentina (February 1960) and Ecuador (1961) belonged to the USSR and that the USA was the object of the exercise.

The use of force without war is often but the prelude to war itself. For example, the small Argentinian landing on the island of South Georgia might have been recorded as a show of force without war, had it not been followed immediately by the South Atlantic War of 1982.

21. Force Without War

The USA started wooing China with military approaches in the mid-1970s. In December 1975, US President Ford approved the sale to China of Rolls-Royce Spey engines and an engine plant by Britain. In October 1976, the US National Security Council approved the sale of two advanced computers with military applications. In February 1980, President Carter's Secretary of Defense, Harold Brown, visited Beijing. In March 1980, *Munitions Control Newsletter* No. 81 specified categories of military equipment which could be considered for sale to China. In June 1981, Alexander Haig, Secretary of State under President Reagan, announced in Beijing that the US would consider selling weapons to China. In April 1982, President Reagan offered to reduce arms sales to Taiwan and to support the reunification of China. In November 1982, the USA placed no obstacles in the way of a £100 million British arms sale to China, although at the time the USA was imposing sanctions on West European suppliers of equipment for the Soviet gasline.

Numbers given for military equipment tell only part of a story: 'China's air force is the service least capable of successfully performing its mission. It consists largely of air defence fighters capable of making intercepts only in good weather during daylight hours. The air force suffers severe deficiencies in avionics, missile systems and jet engines. Moreover, it is the most difficult service to modernize, because the needed technologies are currently beyond China's grasp and are extremely expensive.' *Sydney H. Jamines, CIA*

22. China: The Middle Kingdom

China's development of its nuclear arsenal reached a new level in October 1982, with its first test-launch of a missile from a submarine.

In addition to the forces shown on the map, in 1981 the USA had 200 combat aircraft in Japan, 100 in South Korea and 300 in the Philippines. The USSR had 90 aircraft in Mongolia.

23. Hey, Big Spender
24. The Military Bite

There are four major sources of information on military spending. They are all published annually: *World Military Expenditures and Arms Transfers,* by the US Arms Control and Disarmament Agency (ACDA); *The Military Balance,* by the International Institute of Strategic Studies (IISS); *World Military and Social Expenditures,* compiled by Ruth Leger Sivard; and *World Armaments and Disarmament: SIPRI Yearbook,* produced by the Stockholm International Peace Research Institute (SIPRI). ACDA's figures are official US government figures, provided by the CIA. The other three publications use a variety of sources – UN, NATO, government statistics and press reports – but rework them.

We use SIPRI's figures for *Map 23: Hey, Big Spender,* because they are more up-to-date than those of ACDA or Sivard, and because they are more comprehensive than those of the IISS. SIPRI is an independent institution: whatever biases it may have, they do not derive from any role as an official government mouthpiece. Sivard is also independent and provides more comprehensive information: we use Sivard for *Map 24: The Military Bite* and *Map 25: Goliaths.* But Sivard is not suitable for comparisons from one year to another.

Although SIPRI provides very recent figures for many states and for regional and world totals, we have had to make our own estimates for the military spending of many states during 1981. We did this by extrapolating trends in spending through the 1970s, using SIPRI's regional totals to set the framework. Given the magnitudes involved, and in view of the fundamental problems in all such statistics, the results are quite adequate for a visual comparison.

The basic problems in the statistics fall into two categories. First, there is the problem of reliable reporting. Most states do not publish their own figures annually. Many of the figures given are widely distrusted. Second, there is the problem of finding a basis of comparison. For a start, the definition of military spending varies. Then, figures in national currencies need to be translated into a single currency, usually the US dollar, in order to compare them for a single year. To compare them over a period of years, it is necessary to find a way of eliminating the effects of inflation to show the 'real' increase or decrease in spending. Both tasks are complex. Fluctuations in the figures often result more from fluctuations in the dollar exchange rate than from changes in the actual volume of expenditure. There are several different indices for inflation and the choice of index is important (for example, the index for consumer prices is inappropriate because military goods and services are very different). The year chosen as the base year for calculating the rise and fall of spending is also important and can change the results quite dramatically.

These problems are all magnified in the case of comparisons between the military spending of the USA and its allies on the one hand, and the USSR and its allies on the other. The official Soviet figure is widely thought to be unreliable. The official rouble-dollar exchange rate is artificial and of little help.

In the USA, the CIA has developed a very sophisticated system for translating Soviet military spending into dollars. This ignores the official budget, and instead attempts to calculate the cost to the USA of running the USSR's armed forces. It is essentially artificial, since different things cost different amounts relative to each other in their two societies. US personnel are more expensive than Soviet; US technology tends to be much more sophisticated. The result of the CIA's calculation is that the USSR appears to spend a great deal more on the military than the USA. But the calculation has the weakness that if American costs go up, so too does the CIA's version of the USSR's military budget. Thus, if US soldiers get a pay increase, the perceived Soviet budget goes up accordingly.

Sivard and SIPRI use different techniques, partly based on calculating a supposed 'military' exchange rate. Both find that the USA and USSR spend about the same on their armed forces.

We concluded that the cartogram, because it provides approximate rather than detailed comparisons, would be the most effective and judicious technique for showing international comparison. We advise readers not to try to calculate exactly each state's proportion of the global total. Broad comparisons and contrasts count for much more.

In charting the rate of growth of military spending, we did not include countries in which hyperinflation causes insurmountable statistical problems. We began with 1973 for Bangladesh and 1975 for Mozambique. And in identifying states whose military spending remained stable across the decade, we allowed a margin of error of 5 per cent either way. This reflects the inescapable imprecision in all such comparisons.

General economic data are reported more slowly than that for military spending. We use Sivard's figures for *Map 24: The Military Bite* because they are more comprehensive and include military spending and Gross National Product (GNP) in the same prices. Although Sivard's figures should not be used for comparing military spending over time, they are sufficiently reliable for presenting the proportion of GNP spent on the military.

The contrasts between the power and wealth of the superpowers and the rest of the world are so striking that reservations about the data, though still relevant, are less important than for *Maps 23* and *24*. Sivard was used as the source for this map because it is more comprehensive than SIPRI and because the lag in reporting Gross National Products makes the lesser immediacy of her figures on military spending less important.

25. Goliaths

In the comparisons between the military spending of the superpowers and the GNPs of the rest, three countries straddle the divisions we have used in the colour code. Niger's 1978 GNP was slightly over 1 per cent of Soviet military spending, but slightly under 1 per cent of the USA's; Peru straddles the 10 per cent mark, and Turkey straddles the 50 per cent mark.

In comparing military spending with the military contracts of top US corporations, two points are worth noting. First, the figures for a single year are a snapshot: for example, in 1980 General Dynamics was still the top US contractor but the value of its contracts was several hundred million dollars below its 1978 level. Second, these comparisons are based on contracts with the US Department of Defense; exports are not included.

Military personnel are full-time, uniformed members of the regular armed forces as reported for July 1981 in *The Military Balance 1981-1982*. Excluded are members of paramilitary forces, special forces, covert forces. Medical personnel are physicians on the live register (excluding military physicians), registered midwives, and qualified, assistant and practical nurses as reported for 1977 in *World Health Statistics 1980*. In each case these were the latest figures available at the time of undertaking the research.

26. Under Arms

The figures need to be interpreted cautiously. Medical statistics tend to encompass all the people trained formally in 'western' allopathic medicine and to ignore 'traditional' homeopathic healing and unregistered midwives. Even when the same categories are used, comparisons in different countries between military and medical personnel are not always made on the same basis. The relative size of the military is *overstated* in 22 countries: Afghanistan, Argentina, Brazil, Chad, Chile, Congo, Guyana, Hungary, Ireland, Israel, Malaysia, Mexico, Morocco, Mozambique, Nepal, Oman, Sri Lanka, Tanzania, Tunisia, United Arab Emirates, United Kingdom and Zambia. The reverse is true in eleven countries where the relative size of the military is *understated:* Burma, Denmark, Egypt, Finland, Ghana, Pakistan, Portugal, Singapore, South Africa, Spain, Zimbabwe. The world average is distorted in favour of medical personnel.

Figures for military reserves are the least reliable. They tend to be exaggerated as much by hostile propagandists as by complacent high commands, except in the very few countries where reserves form an essential, quickly-mobilisable force.

The estimates on which this map is based are, in our view, little short of heroic. That is, they represent a series of informed guesses. On the face of it, it is

27. All in a Day's Work

astonishing that such an exercise should be necessary. Yet the total employment provided by the international military order is a subject on which there is very little information.

A United Nations estimate, published in 1977, set the world ratio between non-uniformed and uniformed employment at just under 3:1 – 60 million engaged in military-related work, compared with 22 million in the armed forces. Figures are available from some countries for civil servants. For fewer countries, figures are available for employment in corporations working on military contracts. Figures for employment on sub-contracts are yet patchier.

The most ambitious studies to date are those by Wassily Leontief and Faye Duchin, working at the Institute of Economic Analysis at New York University. They represent an important achievement and we use them for *Map 32: Industrial Muscle* (see below), but they are unfortunately flawed for our purposes here.

The estimates for this map begin with the figures used for *Map 26: Under Arms*, on the size of total armed forces. Using the figures available for some countries, we were able to establish a moderately firm basis for the employment ratio between the economic tail and military teeth in states at or near the apex of the international military order. For other states, we adjusted the ratio to reflect the scale of the arms industry, if any (see *Map 29: The Arms Makers* and *Map 33: Sharing the Spoils*), and random knowledge about the scale of state bureaucracies.

The result is little more than an impressionistic sketch. It does more to indicate a yawning gap in basic knowledge than to fill it. It must be added that military-related employment is in any case rather fluid, as the composition of military spending fluctuates and as contracts are gained and completed. But we believe the results point in the right direction. In the present state of information about the subject, no greater ambition than that is worth entertaining.

28. Shuttle Service The USA and the USSR rely on each other far more than is shown in this map, for beyond the materials that enter into the making of a space shuttle there are the grain and high technology goods that flow in one direction and the other raw materials that flow in the other direction.

South Africa is even more important as a supplier of strategic materials than the inset map suggests. For example, it is a major supplier of uranium to western countries.

Total military consumption of raw materials is not known. But the USA's armed forces alone take more than 40 per cent of world titanium output; 11-14 per cent of aluminium, copper, lead and zinc; and some 10 per cent of a good few others.

The import dependence of the two other major industrial centres of the world is as follows:

	EEC	Japan		EEC	Japan
	percentages			percentages	
Aluminium/Bauxite	74	100	Manganese	99	95
Antimony	95	–	Nickel	99	98
Asbestos	94	98	Platinum group	100	100
Cadmium	100	–	Silver	93	71
Chromium	98	94	Tantalum	100	–
Cobalt	100	100	Tin	88	94
Columbium	100	–	Titanium	100	–
Copper	91	95	Tungsten	99	100
Iron ore	82	99	Vanadium	99	100
Lead	69	78	Zinc	80	69

The relative scale of arms making is shown by the designation of countries as major, medium or minor arms makers. Major arms makers are virtually or actually self-sufficient in designing and producing weapons in all four categories and a range of equipment in each. They are all important arms exporters. Minor arms makers are largely dependent on imports to equip their forces, but do have some production capacity. Their arms manufacturers usually use foreign designs for which they have purchased a production license, although some of these states have a limited design capacity for some weapons. Medium arms makers fall in between. These are states with some development capacity, but usually not for all the equipment they produce. They are self-sufficient in a few types of equipment, import a large proportion of their arms and, with some exceptions, export relatively limited quantities.

29. The Arms Makers

Inevitably there remain great differences within each category — for example between the superpowers and the rest of the major arms makers, or between countries like Norway and Sweden at the top end of the medium arms makers and countries like Singapore and Indonesia at the bottom end.

To provide an overall picture of world arms production, armaments are divided into four categories. Three of them — aerospace, ships and armoured vehicles — are self-explanatory. The fourth is a looser category and encompasses artillery, small arms, shells, bombs and bullets, because some of these are grouped together in our sources.

The two major sources of information on the international arms trade are the Stockholm International Peace Research Institute (SIPRI) and the US Arms Control and Disarmament Agency (ACDA). There are major discrepancies between them. Some can be explained by the fact that SIPRI includes only major weapons in its figures, while ACDA includes all arms shipments, and then again by SIPRI's inclusion of the value of production licenses. Further discrepancies are revealed when figures from either SIPRI or ACDA are compared with the figures provided by exporting states.

30. The Arms Sellers
31. The Arms Buyers

Since the two sets of information cannot be reconciled, we have opted to use SIPRI's, on the grounds that it is an independent institution whereas ACDA is part of the US Department of State. SIPRI's figures are certainly as widely respected and used as those of ACDA — perhaps more so.

Both SIPRI and ACDA exclude the clandestine trade which continues beneath the surface of world affairs. This clandestine trade is not only a matter of purchases by terrorist groups.

All in all, information on the arms trade is especially dubious, which is why SIPRI's own warning on that score is included in *Map 30: The Arms Sellers.* Particular problems attach to figures for arms exports by the USSR; the reasons for this are similar to those which make figures on Soviet military spending so problematic (see note to *Map 23: Hey, Big Spender).*

Although we used SIPRI's information for the market shares of the main exporters, ACDA's was more conveniently arranged for revealing the growing number of *permanent* arms exporters. The period covered by the information on market shares on the map is different from the period covered in the pie chart, and different again from the period covered by the information on the permanent exporters.

SIPRI notes that the scale of Libyan arms exports at the end of the 1970s does not indicate a general trend. Libyan arms exports had previously been very low, but were increased by large re-sales of aircraft and armoured vehicles during 1979. Syria was the major customer. This example also makes the point that it is not necessary to have an arms industry in order to be an arms exporter: second-hand weapons are common in the international arms market.

In *Map 31: The Arms Buyers,* the graph showing third world arms imports by region uses a moving average. This means that the figure given for any year (say 1970) is actually the average for the five-year period in which that is the middle year (thus, 1968-72). This removes sudden fluctuations from one year to another which could be caused by a sudden boost in real trade, but might just as easily be caused by a hiccough in the data. The graph therefore shows the long-term trend of arms imports and that trend is ominously clear.

32. Industrial Muscle The estimates on which this map is based are every bit as heroic as those in *Map 27: All in a Day's Work.* But in this case, the heroism is not ours. Here we utilise the estimates made by Wassily Leontief and Faye Duchin, working at the Institute of Economic Analysis in New York University. Their achievement is to provide some basis on which to assess the distribution of military-industrial output. There are two major flaws. First, their estimates are based on official figures provided by the US Arms Control and Disarmament Agency (ACDA). It is a standard feature of such figures to underestimate the USA relative to the USSR in all things military. They have been caught out on numerous occasions, but the practice continues. Second, though they may satisfy formal economic criteria, Leontief and Duchin collapse the world's states into fifteen regions which have no political or military and little geographic rationale.

We record on the map our suspicions of this comparison of US and Soviet output. But the estimates are probably about right in showing the degree to which output is concentrated in a rather small number of countries. That is, the estimates unmistakably reveal the basic hierarchy of the international military order.

34. War Fair The details of operational performance which would be required for a full evaluation of the weapons used in the South Atlantic war of 1982 remain classified secrets in both Argentina and the UK. Only those two states, any other states with which they share secrets, and the USA (see *Map 12: Star Wars* and *Map 20: The US Network*) can have the information required for a systematic judgement about the effectiveness or ineffectiveness of different weapons. But a great many impressionistic judgements have been made, including some which are probably quite reliable. It is these that we have drawn on to evaluate the performance of weapons.

Costs of weapons are not always easily available. Where they are not in official or other public literature, we were able to glean bits and pieces of information and from these we have made reasonable deductions.

The weapon systems shown in this map do not add up to a comprehensive list of the systems used in the war. Nor are they necessarily the most important. The common soldier's rifle, iron bombs and artillery shells all have an equal claim in that regard. We have, instead, shown the weaponry on which the press focussed its interest.

The Dagger/Nasher, which in the map we show as made in France as well as Israel, is actually *manufactured* only in Israel from a French design.

35. Military Rule Fifty-three of the 160 states for which there is information were ruled by their military forces at some time since the end of the second world war. Thirty-one of these were under military rule in 1981-82.

These were countries in which the military governed directly under edicts promulgated by themselves, and ones which they ruled effectively although indirectly, having adopted the appearance as well as the appurtenances of civilian power. They include countries in which the military have become entrenched in all aspects of civil government (Paraguay) as well as those in which the military authority is foreign (Afghanistan). Not included are: countries wholly or partly under martial law where a renewal of military authority is required; states where the military are very influential but not in control (Israel, Jordan); or where the head of state is a career officer with continuing ties with the military but whose rule does not depend upon them (Guinea, Zaire).

Popular expectations are moulded by hearsay and tradition as well as by direct experience. This is as true of military rule as of any other public arrangement and explains to some extent the recurrence of military rule once it has taken place.

36. The Military as Police The military function as a civil police force in a number of circumstances: where large sections of the population are actively opposed to the government; where the civil police are weak, or demoralised, or suddenly overwhelmed; where the governing classes are faction-ridden and organised around different branches of the state; where a country is under military rule or martial law. The absence of military policing of the general population indicates no more than that these circumstances do not obtain. It says nothing about the state of human rights in the country.

'Violent policing' refers to those activities of armed forces when they confront unarmed and unfocussed opposition. A common example is the use of armies against demonstrators and rioters. These actions may occur as an adjunct to a counter-insurgency war, and the different kinds of confrontation often shade into each other.

Some policing functions frequently undertaken by the military have been ignored: notably the forced repatriation of refugees which occurs commonly in large parts of Africa and South East Asia. We have also left out such activities as providing essential services in the course of a strike.

In determining a country's main army mission we have had to simplify as well as rely on informed judgement. The United Kingdom army, for example, is trained for external war, yet some of its training and most of its recent experience of war – apart from the South Atlantic episode of early 1982 – are as a counter-insurgency force in Northern Ireland.

While no link is intended between an army's domestic mission and 'disappearances', it is nonetheless true that garrison armies are in a favourable position to carry them out.

The USA was responsible for about 80 per cent of the accidents and incidents with nuclear weapons shown on this map. This only shows that more information has been extracted there than anywhere else. Even so, it is far from certain that the list of US accidents and incidents is complete; very little of the information on the map was provided willingly. We are therefore confident that the real number of mishaps is considerably greater.

37. Broken Arrows, Bent Spears

The accidental launchings of nuclear-tipped surface-to-air missiles referred to in the text were authoritatively reported, but without dates or places. The accident record on the Titan intercontinental missiles came to light in the wake of an accident in 1980, when a Titan exploded, hurling its warhead several hundred metres. The information on false alerts in 1979 and 1980 was revealed in a Congressional enquiry into the problem, after an apparent spate of widely publicised false alerts; it became evident that what had previously been public knowledge was only the tip of an iceberg.

There have been other US accidents on which information is incomplete. In 1950, somewhere at sea, an aircraft jettisoned a nuclear bomb. Sometime, somewhere in the Arctic, there was an unspecified accident. In 1968, a Polaris submarine collided with a merchant ship which then sank. US submarines have, at various times, collided with Soviet submarines and with a Vietnamese minesweeper, have surfaced under a Soviet warship and have run aground in Soviet territorial waters. There have also been literally hundreds of crashes by aircraft which normally or occasionally carry nuclear weapons, and which may or may not have had them on board at the time of the crash. This last item, of course, applies to all the states which deploy nuclear weapons.

In providing information about what occurred in each incident, we have shown only the most serious element of the event. Thus, accidents in which there was a fire or explosion followed by a radiation leak are simply shown as having released radiation.

'Broken Arrow' and 'Bent Spear' are US categories. We have applied them to British, French and Soviet accidents. The official definition of a Broken Arrow is an event which involves accidental or unauthorised launching of a weapon, or a nuclear detonation, or a non-nuclear detonation of a nuclear weapon, or burning, or radioactive contamination, or loss or theft of a nuclear weapon, or where there is an actual or implied public hazard. A Bent Spear is an event which involves evident damage to nuclear weapons or components, or which requires immediate safety action, or which could result in an adverse public reaction.

We think the last point is particularly revealing about the official mind.

The military devours huge and increasing quantities of materials (see *Map 24: The Military Bite* and *Map 28: Shuttle Service*). Not only does it spill an ever-increasing proportion of its growing destructive power into the environment, it also claims

38. The Martyred Earth

larger and larger areas for tests and training.

The bigger and more mechanised the army, the more room per soldier does it require for training: an infantry battalion (750 soldiers) needs 1200 hectares for manoeuvres; a brigade (5000 soldiers) needs 18,000 hectares; an armoured division (10-15,000 soldiers with up to 300 armoured vehicles) needs optimally 66,400 hectares. In the USA, the area for training in air-to-ground attack using ordinary bombs is 1500 hectares; when using air-to-ground missiles it is 20,400 hectares. The area for nuclear weapons testing can be immense: the US test of 1954 at Bikini Atoll, Marshall Islands, spread radioactive contamination over more than two million hectares.

The number of US military personnel killed in battle during the second world war, the Korean war and the second Indochina war dropped in the ratio of 15:2:1 per month; and the number of battle deaths among the forces opposed to the US dropped in the same ratio. But US spending on munitions went up in the ratio of 1:5:7; US spending on munitions per enemy soldier killed went up 1:6:18; and the weight of munitions used by the US went up 1:8:26.

During the second world war, 31 per cent of Allied air attacks were 'area bombings' against ill-defined targets, usually urban. During the Korean war, 74 per cent of US air attacks were against even less defined (usually rural) area targets. During the USA's war in Vietnam, 85 per cent of its air attacks were of this nature.

39. Achilles' Heel Reliability is a compound of loyalty and morale. Forces with high morale may be unreliable if they are likely to attempt to take over state power. Armed forces which are unlikely to attempt a *coup* may be unreliable if they suffer from morale problems, whether from low pay, poor conditions, defeat in war or anything else. Different sections of the forces may vary in their attitudes and allegiance.

For this map we sought judgements on the loyalty and morale of as many armed forces as possible. We used a rough three-point scale to classify the evaluations, and then synthesised them into a five-point scale for overall reliability. The result is, inevitably, somewhat impressionistic.

The reliability of the 'other ranks' in a conscript army may be more tenuous than in a volunteer force. When the right to conscientious objection is denied or limited, this increases the degree of coercion involved in conscription. However, the information available, especially outside Europe and North America, is so scarce and outdated that we felt unable to indicate in the map the legal status of conscientious objection. Mexico and Nicaragua both have volunteer regular forces, but Mexico has a conscripted part-time militia, and Nicaragua has provisions for using conscription in an emergency.

40. A New Order? The news media do not specialise in accurate or comprehensive reporting of disarmament movements. It is therefore very possible that this map omits the activities of more than one disarmament movement.

The map also includes three seeming anomalies. In East Germany we show that there was both an official demonstration (autumn 1981) and an independent movement suffering harrassment. This was indeed the case at the end of 1982. In the USSR, a small committee in Moscow began independent disarmament activities in summer 1982. Groups in other cities followed suit. But the independent demonstration that took place there was organised by a group of Scandinavian women who, with official permission, made a peace march into the USSR. In Turkey, early 1982, the entire executive of the Turkish Peace Association was arrested by the military regime, and by the end of the year, no other group had emerged to take its place.

Sources for the Maps

Ambio: a journal of the human environment, Stockholm, Royal Swedish Academy of Sciences, N. 2-3, 1982.

Amnesty International, *Reports*, London, Amnesty International Publications. Annual.

Arkin, W., 'Nuclear weapons in Europe' in Mary Kaldor and Dan Smith, eds, *Disarming Europe*, London, Merlin Press, 1982.

Banks, Arthur S., and William Overstreet, eds, *Political Handbook of the World 1981*, New York and London, McGraw-Hill for the Center for Social Analysis of the State University of New York at Binghamton and for the Council on Foreign Relations, 1981.

Barnett, A. Doak, *China and the Major Powers in East Asia*, Washington DC, Brookings Institution, 1977.

Ball, Desmond, *Can Nuclear War Be Controlled?* London, International Institute for Strategic Studies, 1981. Adelphi Paper 169.

Blechman, Barry M., and Stephen S. Kaplan, *Force Without War: US Armed Forces as a Political Instrument*, Washington DC, Brookings Institution, 1978.

Bonds, Ray, ed, *The Chinese War Machine: A Technical Analysis of the Strategy and Weapons of the People's Republic of China*, London, Salamander Books, 1979.

Breyer, Siegfried, and Norman Polmar, *Guide to the Soviet Navy*, Annapolis, United States Naval Institute Press, 1977 and Cambridge, Patrick Stephens, 1977. 2nd edition.

Brzoska, Michael, Peter Lock and Herbert Wulf, *Rüstungsproduktion in Westeuropa*, Hamburg, Institut für Friedensforschung und Sicherheits Politik (IFSH), Forschungsberichte, Heft 15, Dec 1979.

Bunge, William, 'The geography of nuclear war' manuscript, 1982.

Cable, James, *Gunboat Diplomacy 1919-1979: Political Applications of Limited Naval Force*, London, Macmillan, 1981.

Campbell, Christy, *War Facts Now*, London, Fontana, 1982.

Carver, Michael, *War Since 1945*, London, Weidenfeld & Nicolson, 1980.

Center for Defense Information, *The Defense Monitor*, Washington DC, Vol.IX, No. 1, 1980; Vol. X, No. 5, 1981; Vol. X, No. 8, 1982.

The Chinese Armed Forces Today: The US Defense Intelligence Agency Handbook of China's Army, Navy and Air Force, London, Melbourne, Arms and Armour Press, 1979.

Clutterbuck, Richard, *Riot and Revolution in Singapore and Malaya, 1945-1963*, London, Faber, 1973.

Collins, John, *US-Soviet Military Balance*, New York and London, McGraw-Hill, 1980.

Cornell, R.A., 'National defense stockpile management of industrial minerals' in Coope, B.M., ed, *Industrial Minerals: Proceedings of the 4th Industrial Minerals International Congress* held at the Hilton Hotel, Atlanta Ga., USA, 28-30 May 1980. London, *Metal Bulletin*.

Crowson, Phillip, and Sylvia Francis, *British Foreign Policy to 1985: Non-Fuel Minerals and Policy, Data Base*, [London, Royal Institute of International Affairs, 1978]. Duplicated.

Defense of Japan 1980, [Tokyo] Defense Agency [1980].

Dumas, Lloyd J., 'Human fallibility and weapons', *The Bulletin of the Atomic Scientists*, Nov 1980.

Dunn, Lewis A., *Controlling the Bomb: Nuclear Proliferation in the 1980s*, New Haven and London, Yale University Press, 1982.

Dupuy, R. Ernest, and Trevor N. Dupuy, *The Encyclopedia of Military History from 3500 BC to the present*, London and Sydney, Jane's, 1976. Revised edition.

Dupuy, Trevor N., *Numbers, Predictions and War*, London, MacDonald and Jane's, 1979.

Elliot, Gil, *Twentieth Century Book of the Dead*, London, Allen Lane, 1972.

Enthoven, A.C., and K.W. Smith, *How Much is Enough? Shaping the Defense Program 1961-1969*, New York, Harper & Row, 1971.

The Europa Year Book 1981: A World Survey, London, Europa Publications [1981].

Fairhall, David, *Russia Looks to the Sea: A Study of the Expansion of Soviet Maritime Power*, London, Andre Deutsch, 1971.

Feldman, Shai, *The Raid on Osiraq: A Preliminary Assessment*, [Tel Aviv] Tel Aviv University Center for Strategic Studies, Aug 1981, CSS Memorandum No. 5. Duplicated.

Fine, Daniel I., 'Mineral resource dependency crisis: Soviet Union and United States' in James

Arnold Miller, Daniel I. Fine and R. Daniel McMichael, eds, *The Resource War in 3D – Dependency, Diplomacy, Defense*, Pittsburgh Pa., World Affairs Council of Pittsburgh, 1980.

Gervasi, Tom, *Arsenal of Democracy*, New York, Grove Press, 1982. 2nd edition.
Gilbert, Martin, *The Arab-Israeli Conflict: Its History in Maps*, London, Weidenfeld & Nicolson, 1979. 3rd edition.
Goldblat, Jozef, *Agreements for Arms Control: A Critical Survey*, London, Taylor & Francis, 1982.
Gorshkov, S.G., *The Sea Power of the State*, Oxford, Pergamon Press, 1979.

Harris, R., and J. Paxman, *A Higher Form of Killing*, London, Chatto & Windus, 1982.

Independent Commission on International Development Issues, *North-South: A Programme for Survival*, London, Pan, 1980.
Institute for the Study of Conflict, *Annual of Power and Conflict*, London, ISC. Annual.
International Institute for Strategic Studies, *The Military Balance*, London, IISS. Annual.
International Institute for Strategic Studies, *Strategic Survey*, London, IISS. Annual.

Jane's All the World's Aircraft, London, Jane's. Annual.
Jane's Armour and Artillery, London, Jane's. Annual.
Jane's Fighting Ships, London, Jane's. Annual.
Jane's Infantry Weapons, London, Jane's. Annual.
Jane's Weapon Systems, London, Jane's. Annual.
Jasani, Bhupendra, ed, *Outer Space: A New Dimension of the Arms Race*, London, Taylor & Francis, 1982.

Kaplan, Stephen S., *Diplomacy of Power: Soviet Armed Forces as a Political Instrument*, Washington DC, Brookings Institution, 1981.
Keegan, John, *World Armies*, London, Macmillan, 1979.
Kende, Istvan, 'Twenty-five years of local wars', *Journal of Peace Research*, Vol. VIII, No. 1, 1971.
Kende, Istvan, 'Wars of ten years' (1967-76), *Journal of Peace Research*, Vol. XV, No. 3, 1978.
Kidron, Michael, and Ronald Segal, *The State of the World Atlas*, London, Pan, 1981 and Heinemann Educational Books, 1981; New York, Simon & Schuster, 1981.
Klare, M.T., *Beyond the Vietnam Syndrome*, Washington DC, Institute for Policy Studies, 1981.
Klare, M.T., and C. Arnson, *Supplying Repression*, Washington DC, Institute for Policy Studies, 1981.
Kurian, George Thomas, *Encyclopedia of the Third World*, London, Mansell, 1979. 2 vols.

Lanir, Zvi, *Israel's Involvement in Lebanon: A Precedent for an 'Open' Game with Syria?* [Tel Aviv] Tel Aviv University Center for Strategic Studies, Paper No. 10, Apr 1981.
Leitenberg, M., R. Kalish and D. Lombardi, *A Survey of Studies of Post World War II Wars, Conflicts and Military Coups*, Ithaca NY, Cornell University Press, 1977.
Leontief, Wassily, and Faye Duchin, *Worldwide Economic Implications of a Limitation on Military Spending*. Prepared for the UN Centre for Disarmament, Contract No. CTR OI. New York, New York University, Institute for Economic Analysis, Jun 1980. Duplicated.
Leontief, Wassily, and Faye Duchin, *Worldwide Implications of Hypothetical Changes in Military Spending (An Input-Output Approach)*. Contract No. AC8WC117. Prepared for US Arms Control and Disarmament Agency. New York, New York University, Institute for Economic Analysis, Aug 1980. Duplicated.
Lewy, Guenter, *America in Vietnam*, New York, Oxford University Press, 1978.
Lock, Peter, and Herbert Wulf, *Register of Arms Production in Developing Countries*, Hamburg, Arbeitsgruppe Rüstung und Unterentwicklung 1977. Duplicated.

Mickolous, Edward F., *Transnational Terrorism: A Chronology of Events, 1968-79*, London, Aldwych Press, 1980.
Mineral Economics Symposium, 6th 1980, George Washington University. 'US minerals issues. The seventies: a review', American Institute of Mining, Metallurgical and Petroleum Engineers, published as Vol. 5, No. 1, 1981 of *Materials and Society*, Oxford, Pergamon Press, 1981.
Moore, Captain John E., *The Soviet Navy Today*, London, MacDonald & Jane's, 1975.
Morgan, John D. jr, 'Minerals from a strategic viewpoint' in Mineral Economics Symposium, *op. cit.*

NARMIC (National Action/Research on the Military Industrial Complex) 'The Defense Department's Top 100', Philadelphia Pa., NARMIC.
NARMIC (National Action/Research on the Military Industrial Complex), *The Military-Industrial Atlas of the United States*, Philadelphia Pa., NARMIC, 1981.
National Science Foundation, *Federal Funds for Research and Development: Fiscal Years 1979, 1980 and 1981*, Washington DC, NSF, 1980.

Plascov, Avi, *A Palestinian State? Examining the Alternatives*, London, International Institute for Strategic Studies, 1981. Adelphi Paper 163.

Richardson, Lewis F., *Statistics of Deadly Quarrels*, edited by Quincy Wright and C.C. Lienan, Pittsburgh Pa., The Boxwood Press, and Chicago, Quadrangle Books, 1960.

Sassoon, Enrico, 'Materie prime e politica estera: i paese OCSE di fronte al rischio della interruzione delle furniture di materie prime strategiche', *L'Industria Mineraria*, Vol. 11, No. 1, Jan-Feb 1981.
Scott, Harriet Fast, and William F. Scott, *The Armed Forces of the USSR*, Boulder Co., Westview Press, 1979.
Segal, Gerald, ed, *The China Factor*, London, Croom Helm, 1982.
Segal, Gerald, 'China's nuclear posture for the 1980s', *Survival* XXIII, No. 1, Jan-Feb 1981.
Segal, Gerald, 'China's security debate', *Survival*, Mar-Apr 1982.
Singer, J. David, and Melvin Small, *The Wages of War 1816-1965: A Statistical Handbook*, New York and London, John Wiley, 1972.
Sivard, Ruth Leger, *World Military and Social Expenditures*, Leesburg Va., World Priorities. Annual.
Smith, Colin, and John Andrews, *The Palestinians*, [London] Minority Rights Group, 1979. 3rd edition. Report No. 24.
Stockholm International Peace Research Institute, *The Problem of Chemical and Biological Warfare*, Stockholm, Almqvist & Wiksell. Vol. 1, *The Rise of CB Weapons*, 1971.
Stockholm International Peace Research Institute, *Warfare in a Fragile World: Military impact on the Human Environment* by Arthur H. Westing, London, Taylor & Francis, 1980.
Stockholm International Peace Research Institute, *World Armaments and Disarmament: SIPRI Yearbook*, London, Taylor & Francis. Annual. To 1977, published in Stockholm by Almqvist & Wiksell.
Sutton, Antony C., *Wars and Revolutions: A Comprehensive List of Conflicts, including Fatalities*, Stanford Ca., Hoover Institution on War, Revolution and Peace, July 1971. Part One: 1820 to 1900; Part Two: 1900 to 1972. Duplicated in 50 copies.
Suvorov, Viktor, *pseud., The Liberators: Inside the Soviet Army*, London, Hamish Hamilton, 1981.

Tajima, Takashi, *China and South-East Asia: Strategic Interests and Policy Prospects*, London, International Institute for Strategic Studies, 1981. Adelphi Paper 172.
Tan Eng Bok, Georges, 'La Stratégie nucléaire chinoise', *Stratégique* 1980, No.7.

United Kingdom, *The Falklands Campaign: The Lessons,* London, HMSO, Dec 1982, Cmnd. 8758.
United Kingdom, *Statement on the Defence Estimates 1982*, London, HMSO, 1982. Cmnd. 8259-I.
United Nations, General Assembly. *Economic and Social Consequences of the Armaments Race and Its Extremely Harmful Effects on World Peace and Security. Report of the Secretary General*, 12 Aug 1977, New York, UN, 1977. A/32/88 and *Addendum* 12 Sept 1977, A/32/88 Add. 1.
United Nations, *Yearbook of National Accounts Statistics 1979*, New York, UN, 1980. 2 vols.
United States, Arms Control and Disarmament Agency, *World Military Expenditures and Arms Transfers*, Washington DC, USGPO, 1982. Annual.
United States, Bureau of Mines, *Minerals Yearbook 1980*, Washington DC, USGPO, 1982. 2 vols.
United States Central Intelligence Agency, *The World Factbook – 1981*, Washington DC, CIA National Foreign Assessment Center, Apr 1981.
United States Congress, House of Representatives Committee on Foreign Affairs, *Israeli Attack on Iraqi Nuclear Facilities*, Hearings before the Subcommittees on International Security and Scientific Affairs on Europe and the Middle East and on International Economic Policy and Trade, 97th Congress, 1st Session, 17 and 25 June 1981.
United States Congress, House of Representatives Committee on Foreign Affairs, Subcommittee on Africa, *The Possibility of a Resource War in Southern Africa*, Hearings 8 July 1981, Washington DC, USGPO, 1981.
United States Congress, House of Representatives Committee on Foreign Affairs Print, *Chronologies of Major Developments in Selected Areas of Foreign Affairs 1981*. Cumulative edition.
United States Congress, House of Representatives Committee on International Relations, Special Subcommittee on Investigations, *The Palestinian Issue in the Middle East*, Hearings 1975, Washington DC, USGPO, 1976.
United States Congress, Office of Technology Assessment, *The Effects of Nuclear War*, Montclair NJ, Allanheld, Osmun, 1980 and London, Croom Helm, 1980.
United States Congress, Senate Committee on Foreign Relations and Congressional Research Service, *Implications of US-Chinese Military Cooperation*, 97th Congress, 1st Session, Jan 1982.

United States Congress, Senate Committee on Government Affairs, and House of
    Representatives Committee on Foreign Affairs, *Nuclear Proliferation Factbook*,
    96th Congress, 2nd Session, Joint Committee Print, Washington DC, USGPO, 1980.
United States Congressional Budget Office, *Strategic Command, Control and
    Communications: Alternative Approaches for Modernization*, Washington DC, CBO,
    Oct 1981.
United States Congressional Research Service (Foreign Affairs and National Defense
    Division), *United States Foreign Policy and Overseas Military Installations*, Washington DC,
    USGPO, Apr 1979.
United States Council on Environmental Quality and Department of State, *The Global 2000
    Report to the President, Entering the Twenty-First Century*, Harmondsworth,
    Penguin, 1982.
United States Defense Intelligence Agency, *Review of the Soviet Ground Forces*,
    Washington DC, USGPO, 1982.
United States Department of Defense, *Annual Report of Fiscal Year 1982*, Washington DC,
    DOD, 1981.
United States Department of Defense, *Soviet Military Power*, Washington DC, DOD, 1981.
United States Organisation of the Joint Chiefs of Staff, *United States Military Posture for
    FY 1982*, Washington DC, DOD, 1981.
United States Organisation of the Joint Chiefs of Staff, *United States Military Posture for
    FY 1983*, Washington DC, DOD, 1982.

Weinberger, Caspar W. *Statement Before the Senate Armed Services Committee*,
    4 Mar 1981, Washington DC, DOD, 1981.
White, W.D., *US Tactical Air Power*, Washington DC, Brookings Institution, 1974.
Wilkinson, David, *Deadly Quarrels, Lewis F. Richardson and the Statistical Study of War*,
    Berkeley, University of California Press, 1980.
Wit, Joel S., 'Advances in anti-submarine warfare' *Scientific American*, Vol. 244, No. 2,
    Feb 1981.
World Bank, *1981 World Bank Atlas*, Washington DC, International Bank for Reconstruction
    and Development, 1982.
World Health Statistics 1980: Health Personnel and Hospital Establishments, Geneva,
    World Health Organisation, 1980.

In addition we have had access to the research files at the Institute of Policy Studies (IPS),
Washington DC and the Stockholm International Peace Research Institute (SIPRI), and to the
latter's computer-stored data.